Phil & Mic
To Your Financial
Freedom!

Mark

COUNTDOWN TO FINANCIAL FREEDOM

Your Path to a More Meaningful, Active, and Vibrant Retirement

MARK AVALLONE

BALBOA
PRESS
A DIVISION OF HAY HOUSE

Copyright © 2016 Potomac Wealth Advisors, LLC.

All rights reserved. No part of this book may be used or reproduced by any means, graphic, electronic, or mechanical, including photocopying, recording, taping or by any information storage retrieval system without the written permission of the author except in the case of brief quotations embodied in critical articles and reviews.

Balboa Press books may be ordered through booksellers or by contacting:

Balboa Press
A Division of Hay House
1663 Liberty Drive
Bloomington, IN 47403
www.balboapress.com
1 (877) 407-4847

Because of the dynamic nature of the Internet, any web addresses or links contained in this book may have changed since publication and may no longer be valid. The views expressed in this work are solely those of the author and do not necessarily reflect the views of the publisher, and the publisher hereby disclaims any responsibility for them.

The information, ideas, and suggestions in this book are not intended to render professional advice. Before following any suggestions contained in this book, you should consult your personal accountant or other financial advisor. Neither the author nor the publisher shall be liable or responsible for any loss or damage allegedly arising as a consequence of your use or application of any information or suggestions in this book.

Mark Avallone is a registered representative and an investment advisory representative of H. Beck, Inc., Member FINRA/SIPC. H. Beck, Inc. is not affiliated with Potomac Wealth Advisors, LLC. The views, opinions, and strategies expressed by the author and those providing comments are theirs alone and do not necessarily reflect the views, opinions, and strategies of H. Beck, Inc. H. Beck, Inc., makes no representations as to the accuracy, completeness, or suitability of the information provided and will not be liable for any errors, omissions, or damages arising from its use.

There are risks involved with investing, including possible loss of principal. Investments will fluctuate and may be worth more or less than when originally purchased. Diversification and asset allocation may reduce some risks of investing, but do not guarantee a profit or ensure against a loss in a declining market. They are methods used to manage risk. There is no assurance that any particular strategy will work under all market conditions.

Financial advisors do not provide specific tax/legal advice, and this information should not be considered as such. You should always consult a tax/legal advisor regarding your specific tax/legal situation.

Print information available on the last page.

ISBN: 978-1-5043-6190-3 (sc)
ISBN: 978-1-5043-6192-7 (hc)
ISBN: 978-1-5043-6191-0 (e)

Library of Congress Control Number: 2016912013

Balboa Press rev. date: 10/17/2016

Acknowledgements

This book is the result of decades of conversations and helping people with their financial planning. I am fortunate to have worked with many clients who have given me their trust. Their confidence in my ability to help them have a better financial life is very important to me and provides the motivation to put in the long hours required in our business. Along those lines, I want to recognize the great support of my entire team including John Orem, Mark Schlossenberg, Gina Carreira, and Courtney Taylor.

Since starting in the financial industry I have benefitted from working with great people at The Private Bank at Bank of America, SunTrust, and my colleagues at The University of Maryland. I would like to specifically mention the valuable industry insight I have received from Ross Perry, Geoff Sipes, and Todd Taskey, and I want to express my gratitude to Matt Halloran of Top Advisor Coaching and to Lisa Robinson for all her guidance and unwavering belief in my ability to help others.

I want to be sure to thank all those who agreed to be interviewed for this book, to my compliance department who worked many hours on this effort, to my editors, and to Balboa Publishing all of whom made this effort possible. And I want to recognize Dan Janal, Tara Price, Kate Epstein, Melissa Wilson, and Becky Blanton for their important contributions.

Personal and professional friendships are so important and I want to let Lane Cooper, Ben Katz, Jack Rushing, Howard Adler, and Jeff Miller know how much I appreciate all the times they have offered valuable advice. I am also grateful to new friends like Robin Sachs, Sandra Schwartzman, and RMR Associates whose expertise has helped immensely.

Most importantly, I want to acknowledge my wife Christine for all of her insight and support on this project. Finally I want to thank my daughter Abigail who has tolerated her father looking at a computer screen far more than he should have been this past year.

Why I wrote this book...

So many Americans are working hard and yet feel that their financial goals seem out of reach. With this book, I wanted to go beyond the usual canned advice that simply talks about a few investment products and then tells you "what to do." My goal is to provide a comprehensive resource in plain language that describes the current economic challenges facing the middle class while also offering strategies for all phases of your financial life. Armed with this insight, I believe you will be better prepared to chart your financial map, stay on course, and arrive at your destination.

Each person's path to financial freedom is unique. Please take from this book those elements that apply to your individual situation and goals. I trust you'll find it an easy, enjoyable, and helpful read.

Wishing you a confident, informed, and fun financial journey,

Mark

Mark Avallone, MBA, CFP®, CRPS®

Table of Contents

Chapter 1. Million-Dollar Poverty 1
    Millionaire Misconception 1
    Middle-Class Poverty and Million-Dollar Poverty 3
    Sustainable Withdrawal Rate 6
    Charles and Leslie Dougherty 8
    Patti Morton 11
    The Middle-Class Challenge 12

Chapter 2. The Middle-Class Challenge 17
    A Brush with "Middle-Class Poverty" 18
    What Is a Middle-Class Income? 19
    Why the Strength of the Middle Class Matters 25
    Basic Steps and Protections 27
    Just a Crisis Away 28
    Discipline Pays Off: An Inspiring Story 31
    Pensions Are Great If You Have One 32
    Go Get a Pension 34
    Retirement Isn't Cheap 35
    The Magnitude of the Challenge 37
    So What Am I Advocating? 39

Chapter 3. What Is Your Unique Formula™? 41
A Formula Focus 41
Step 1: Determine Your Current Retirement Savings (CRS) 42
Step 2: Determine Your Monthly Savings (MS) 42
    Take-home Pay 42
    Monthly Expenses 43
    Monthly Discretionary Income 43
    Monthly Savings 44
Step 3: Estimate Any Expected Inheritance (EI)................................45
Step 4: Calculate Estimated Assets at Retirement (EAR) 48
Step 5: Calculate your Projected Retirement Income.......................49
Step-by-step Summary..50
Applying the Formula...51
Are You on Track? 52
Behind on Your Goals? 53
Examples of Smart Planning..55
Summary 57

Chapter 4. Four Hurdles on Your Path to Financial Freedom.. 59
Hurdle #1: Stagnant Wages and Underemployment.........................59
Hurdle #2: Rising Costs of Health Care 65
Hurdle #3: An Increasing Tax Burden... 68
Hurdle #4: A Rising Cost of Living..75
    The Rule of 72...76
    Low Interest Rates Are Creating Distortions 81
Summary 83

Chapter 5. Avoiding the Middle-Class Traps (EASY) 87
- E = Entitlement 89
- A = Aspirational Purchases..................92
- S = Short-Term Thinking 94
- Y = Yes to Everything 97
- Summary: The Proactive Saver and Next Steps 101

Chapter 6. Avoiding the Four Enemies of the Investor: BITE 103
- B = Bear Markets 103
  - *But what if you have no pension?..................109*
  - *What if you're young?..................110*
- I = Inflation 110
- T = Taxes..................112
- E = Emotion..................114
- Summary 116

Chapter 7. Avoiding the Financial Devastation of the Three Ds 119
- Disability..................119
  - *"Any Occupation" Versus "Own Occupation"..................123*
  - *Drawbacks to Group Disability Income Coverage..................124*
  - *Who Should Own Their Own Disability Income Policy?..................125*
- Divorce 128
- Death 132
- Summary 135

Chapter 8. 401 Not OK 137

    The Decline of Pensions in America...139

    The Shift to Defined Contribution Plans..141

    Limits and Shortfalls of Defined Contribution 401(k) Plans.........144

    The Catch-Up Provision..146

    The Challenge for Plan Providers and Investors............................147

    Maxing Out Your 401(k) May Still Not Be Enough........................150

    How Much Will Be Enough?...151

    The Taxation of Defined Contribution 401(k) Plans and Social Security 154

    Roth Provisions Inside 401(k) Plans and Roth IRAs......................156

    How Can You Improve Your 401(k)?..158

    The Biggest 401(k) Trap to Avoid 159

    Summary 160

Chapter 9. Countdown to Financial Freedom.................. 163

    In Your 20s..163

    In Your 30s..171

    In Your 40s 179

    In Your 50s..182

    In Your 60s 186

    Summary 190

Chapter 10. What's Next?..191
    Have a Written Financial Plan..193
    Have a Good Savings and Spending Plan and Stick to It.................193
    Painless Savings 195
    Understand How Money Can Work For or Against You: The Impact of Compound Interest 196
        Interest *196*
        How Compound Interest Works... *197*
    The Results of Not Funding Your Retirement...................199
    A Call to Action 200

Appendices

    Calculation to Determine
    What is Your Unique Formula?... 203
        Key Variables:... *203*
        5 Step Process for Determining What is Your Unique Formula?™ *204*
    Sample Cash Flow Worksheet... 207

CHAPTER 1

Million-Dollar Poverty

Millionaire Misconception

If you ask a group of baby boomers, "Who is the first millionaire you ever heard of?" there's a good chance they'll say, "Batman." As we know, Batman, under his famous black cape, was really Bruce Wayne. He was the only son of Dr. Thomas and Mrs. Martha Wayne, two very wealthy and charitable socialites living in Gotham City. Bruce was brought up in a happy, wealthy, and privileged lifestyle in Wayne Manor until he was 8 years old when his parents were killed by a small-time criminal. After his parents' death, Bruce vowed revenge on all things evil—that mostly included members of Gotham's criminal underworld. What helped make his promise of revenge possible was the fortune he inherited from his wealthy parents. Bruce's wealth provided him with the necessary seclusion (i.e., the Batcave), physical means (e.g., crime fighting equipment, crime labs, Batmobile), and flexible schedule (no 9-to-5 job in a cubicle for Batman) he needed in order to fight crime. So what's Batman got to do with the middle class? Plenty.

A million dollars back in 1939, when the comic book character first appeared, was an enormous amount of money. Even well into the 1960s and 1970s, when the Batman television series was at its height, having a million dollars seemed like the answer to all of life's financial struggles. Most Americans never imagined they could accumulate a million dollars, let alone need that much to retire. The world was a less expensive place to live, and many people had reliable lifetime pensions once they retired. In today's world, however, millionaire Bruce Wayne might be just another affluent, upper-middle-class guy facing the challenge of enjoying life while not running out of money at some point.

This is because being a millionaire or having a million dollars in your various accounts—checking, savings, investments, 401(k) plans, and so on—may not be enough to maintain an affluent or even a middle-class lifestyle. You may not own a car as cool as the Batmobile, wear a leather cape, or live in Wayne Manor luxury, but if you are accustomed to a middle-class or affluent lifestyle during your working years, you may need *more* than a million dollars in order to continue the same lifestyle during retirement. If you are young or even approaching middle age, adjusting for increases in the cost of living over the next 20 years or longer, you may need *several* million dollars at retirement in order to remain middle class. If you are still of the mindset that, in 20 or 30 years, $1 million will buy you a middle class retirement, you might be very disappointed. In the future, the income generated off of $1 million may not be able to cover even a lower-middle-class budget! That is what I refer to as "Million-Dollar Poverty."

Unfortunately, most of us will not inherit anything like stately Wayne Manor or millions of dollars from a well-to-do family. The fact is the vast majority of us will be solely responsible for accumulating the millions of dollars needed to maintain the middle-class or affluent lifestyle we have achieved or aspire to achieve. The good news is with a solid understanding of your current financial state and a commitment to create and follow a well-thought-out plan, you can begin to visualize the financial freedom you want. You'll see the term "financial freedom" a lot throughout this book. For many people, and for the purposes of this book, financial freedom is the ability to work only because you *want* to, and not because you have to. Accumulating enough assets to allow for that freedom is the challenge millions of Americans face.

Middle-Class Poverty and Million-Dollar Poverty

I use the term "Middle-Class Poverty" to describe the unwanted, dramatic drop in lifestyle experienced by some middle-class or upper-middle-class retirees, due to the lack of adequate investment income to sustain their lifestyle through their retirement years. When this happens to a family with $1 million or more of investable assets, I call it "Million-Dollar Poverty."

> If you have saved $1 million, is that enough to avoid "Middle-Class Poverty" during retirement?

Let's say you've saved $1 million. That may sound like enough to enjoy your financial freedom, but as I will explain in detail later, applying a 4% withdrawal rate to your $1 million generates only about $40,000. You can also hopefully consider additional social security income—but even so, will that be enough to afford your desired lifestyle? If you are a current retiree, the $40,000 plus your social security payments may amount to a reasonable income, especially if you have a home with no debt and a modest lifestyle. But for future generations, after considering the impact of inflation, this may not be the case.

Let's look at what retiring with $1 million might mean for a young baby boomer, a Gen Xer, and a Millennial.

- **Baby boomer:** If you are 52 and you estimate retiring in 15 years (at age 67) with $1 million saved, when we adjust for a hypothetical 3% average annual inflation rate, your $1 million will be worth about $641,861 in today's dollars. Using a 4% withdrawal rate, your $641,861 will generate only $25,674 in today's purchasing power for your first year of retirement. (Note: if you stick to a 4% withdrawal rate, your actual withdrawal amount may increase or decrease, as the invested amount in your account will fluctuate. But using a 4% withdrawal rate is a good rule of thumb.)

- **Gen Xer:** If you are 42 and estimate retiring in 25 years (age 67) with $1 million saved, it will be worth even less. Adjusted for that same hypothetical 3% average annual inflation rate, your $1 million will be worth only $477,605 in today's dollars at retirement. Using a 4% withdrawal rate, your $477,605 generates only $19,104 in today's purchasing power in your first year of retirement!

- **Millennial:** If you are 32 and estimate retiring in 35 years (age 67), then your $1 million will be worth far less. Adjusted for the same 3% average annual inflation rate, your $1,000,000 will only be worth $355,383 in today's dollars at retirement. Using a 4% withdrawal rate, your $355,383 generates only $14,215 in your first year of retirement as measured by today's purchasing power!

So you can see why I call it "Million-Dollar Poverty" and how it can be a reality, especially for younger people. Let's say you are 32 and want to retire on an income equivalent of $80,000 in today's dollars (not counting social security). Adjusting for an average annual 3% inflation rate over the next 35 years, your $80,000 of income will be worth about $28,430 in today's dollars. Therefore, at retirement, in order to live off an inflation-adjusted income of $80,000, you will need to generate an income of about $225,109 in your first year of retirement. And how much money, using a withdrawal rate of 4% is needed to generate your target income of $225,109? The answer is a whopping $5,627,725! And this is just to retire into an inflation-adjusted, middle-class income of $80,000. For families who have been living on a combined household income greater than $80,000, their need to save may be even higher if they want to maintain their current lifestyle.

Table A. Value of $1 Million for People Retiring at Age 67 Using a 4% Sustainable Withdrawal Rate

Current Age	Amount of Assets at Retirement Age 67	Present Value of Assets at Retirement Age Assuming a 3% Inflation Rate	First Year Income Generated in Today's Dollars
67	$1,000,000	$1,000,000	$40,000
52	$1,000,000	$ 641,861	$25,674
42	$1,000,000	$ 477,605	$19,104
32	$1,000,000	$ 355,383	$14,215

These hypothetical examples demonstrate the impact of inflation and the magnitude of the challenge for younger people. Remember: the future level of purchasing power generated by $1 million can decline every year, and eventually you may need to be a multimillionaire in order to remain in the middle class at retirement. It's hard to visualize a multimillionaire struggling to maintain a middle-class lifestyle, but this may well be the case in the future. This idea of Million-Dollar Poverty comes as a surprise to a lot of people; however, once they get a sound plan in place, they get a better sense of the concept and express relief in seeing that they can plan and try to avoid it.[1]

Sustainable Withdrawal Rate

Earlier, I noted that having $1 million today in retirement could generate $40,000. How did I arrive at this figure? I used the "4 Percent Rule." Widely attributed to financial planner William Bengen, who first wrote about it in 1994, the rule states, in simplified terms, that 4% is a rate at which to withdraw annually from your investments without running out of money throughout your retirement. Let's apply the 4 Percent Rule, and let's assume your money remains invested during retirement in a diversified portfolio while you are withdrawing from your accounts. In this case, $1 million can generate $40,000 of income in the first year (considering market conditions, rates of

---

[1] Examples provided herein are for informational purposes only. They do not reflect actual results and are not guarantees of future results. Actual results will vary and fluctuate with market conditions. These examples assume that your asset allocation remains constant throughout retirement and does not become more conservative as you grow older. Also, these examples do not model the tax consequences or other costs of rebalancing the portfolio. These examples do not take into account any state and/or federal taxes that you would owe upon your withdrawal. Results may vary with each individual. All investments involve risk. Be aware that fluctuations in the financial markets and other factors may cause declines in the value of your account. There is no guarantee that any particular asset allocation or mix of funds will meet your investment objectives or provide you with a given level of income. Therefore, it is important to examine your portfolio under a variety of different return conditions.

return, and other factors that potentially affect future amounts). While you are withdrawing money, it is important that your assets stay invested; otherwise you would be withdrawing principal and rapidly depleting your account value. Market conditions, changes in your asset allocation, and the timing of your retirement (e.g., if you retire just before a market crash) can change your individual results; but overall, 4% is a good place to start when considering how much income your portfolio can generate.

Since Bengen first wrote about a 4% sustainable withdrawal rate to fund a 30-year retirement, subsequent research has backed it up. For example, the 1998 "Trinity Study," so called after Trinity University where it was conducted, closely replicated Bengen's findings. The Trinity Study tested stock/bond mixes under various historical market conditions and concluded, in simplified terms, that 4% is a sustainable withdrawal rate that will maximize income during retirement over 30 years. (This is based on historical data and is no guarantee of any future rate of return for each specific example.)

Another study in 2015 further reinforced the 4 Percent Rule. Applying Mr. Bengen's asset allocation of 50% stocks and 50% intermediate-term government bonds, and analyzing the results over 60 rolling, 30-year periods between 1926 and 2014, the study generated similar results to those of the Bengen and Trinity studies. Of these 60 rolling, 30-year periods, the number of times that a withdrawal rate of 5% allowed an investor to avoid running out of money was only 68%. This is hardly high enough to give an aging retiree a lot of comfort. However, with 30-year time horizons and a 50% stock and 50% bond allocation, the success rate was 100% with a 4% initial withdrawal rate.[2] These results show that unless you expect to die within a few years or are willing to risk running out of money, you should target no more than a 4% withdrawal rate from your retirement assets.

Metaphorically, a sustainable withdrawal rate is like the "two-drink limit," the common sense credence that it's wise to limit yourself to only one or two drinks before getting behind the wheel of a car. Drinking more than that could put your (or someone else's) physical life in peril. Similarly, withdrawing more than 4% per year in retirement could potentially put your or your family's financial life in peril!

My goal in this book is to educate those of you who are striving to attain financial freedom. Understanding the amount of money you will need to retire, the impact of inflation and taxes, and the concept of *sustainable withdrawal rate* are essential to identifying how you will achieve and maintain financial freedom. Applying the concepts in this book can help you prepare for a sound financial future. In this book, I offer examples of people who, in the face of challenges, were able to apply sound strategies and achieve their goals. I also describe how others fell short. Below are two stories I think you'll find interesting.

Charles and Leslie Dougherty

Charles and Leslie Dougherty are an upper-middle-class couple who live, well, wherever they want. While I have not had the pleasure of working with the Doughertys, I am impressed with their personal story.

---

[2] Pfau, Wade. (10 June 2015). *Safe withdrawal rates for retirement and the Trinity Study.* Forbes. Retrieved from http://www.forbes.com/sites/wadepfau/2015/06/10/safe-withdrawal-rates-for-retirement-and-the-trinity-study/#3d52b9ce1c5f

After years of careful planning and following a well-developed savings and investment strategy, they were able to retire somewhat early when Charles turned 50. Their plan was to live off their savings and investments until they hit the "official retirement age" of 65, when they would start drawing on pensions, investments, and 401(k) savings.

To kick off retirement, they bought a live-aboard sailboat, gave up their condo, car, and furniture, and never looked back. They sailed the waters of the Chesapeake Bay, the Caribbean, and the Intracoastal Waterway from Annapolis to Florida for 15 years. But this story doesn't only have Charles and Leslie sailing carefree into the sunset. Unfortunately, they hit rough waters a few years into their adventures when they found that unexpected expenses and some extravagant lifestyle choices were critically jeopardizing their nest egg.

Charles holds an MBA degree and is an engineer, lawyer, and author of 17 fiction and nonfiction books. He considers himself well versed in personal finance strategy, but even he admits that inflation, stock market declines, and unexpected expenses caught him off guard. He hadn't planned, for instance, on the need to spend $5,000 for a broken navigation system for the sailboat. Furthermore, he and Leslie didn't realize they were spending more than $2,000 per month dining out at pricey marina restaurants. They were making excessive withdrawals from their savings in order to cover these and other expenses that fell outside the careful planning they had put in place years before. In a nutshell, the Doughertys were not adhering to a sustainable withdrawal rate. To compound matters, a decline in the stock market meant slower growth in their investments than they had anticipated. The Doughertys were at risk of running out of retirement funding too early. Once they took time to consider this reality, they were very concerned.

Charles and Leslie understood that their ability to adapt in the present would pay off in the future. With some forethought, creativity, and discipline they found ways to reduce spending while not having to compromise too much on their lifestyle. Instead of the $5,000 navigation system, they bought a $1,000 depth finder that met their needs. They better managed their monthly cash flow and started cooking more at home—it cost less than going out, and it was a fun way to spend time together. Once Charles and Leslie took the time to understand the concept of *sustainable withdrawal rate*, it was easier for them to remain disciplined and committed to their plan.

Soon after, the Doughertys' retirement plan was back on track. With continued commitment to their new strategy, they were able to resume living the retirement of their dreams. After living for 15 years on their boat, they decided that, while they would continue to sail occasionally, it was time to buy a car and tour the country sight-seeing and visiting friends and family, especially their six grandchildren—which they now do often and without worrying about how to fund their trips!

The Doughertys don't consider themselves to be rich, but they do consider themselves financially free. As a couple, they started saving and investing early and remained committed to a well-thought-out financial plan, even adjusting their strategies when needed. Thanks to sound planning principles—that we will cover later in this book—the Doughertys have been able to afford to keep life's pleasures rolling during retirement.

The Doughertys' story can be a reminder to younger couples that if you start early and focus on your goals, you have a better chance of reaching them. Their experiences also show us that a couple needs to anticipate potential obstacles at every step of their financial life. This is true even later in life when you are drawing down on your assets (the *distribution phase*).

Retirement planning is not an exact science, even for the most educated among us. Especially in light of all of the economic challenges Millennials and Gen Xers will face in order to remain middle class, let alone affluent, there is a heightened need to make a commitment and develop the discipline to save and remain on plan. Families should be prepared to get creative with their spending choices—and also be prepared to make some tough decisions in order to afford the lifestyle that they will want in retirement.

Patti Morton

Patti Morton is a former Dallas Cowboys marketing manager and widow of Nathan Morton, a former CEO of CompUSA. I have not worked with Patti, but I was impressed when I heard her story. At the peak of his career, Patti's husband, Nathan, died unexpectedly, just as he was about to take his company public. Unfortunately, Nathan did not have a personal financial plan in place when he died, and at the time, Patti did not have a career to fall back on. She was in her mid-40s and faced a new reality without Nathan and without the financial cushion and guidance that a sound financial plan would have supplied. Like many other widows (and newly divorced women), Patti had to rebuild her financial future. She went back to work and reinvented her career. In time, and thanks to her determination, she gained her own professional success and remained committed to a spending, saving, and investment strategy. By having the discipline to stick with her plan and employing sound principles, she was able to reach a more comfortable financial footing and get back to doing many of the things she loved.

Patti fell victim to her spouse's unexpected death—one of the three Ds (divorce, disability, and death) that I cover later in this book. She's not alone. Each year, millions of people living a comfortable middle-class lifestyle suffer one or more of these setbacks. As a result, they often experience a major, undesired change in their income and lifestyle. Patti's story is a reminder that no one is immune to the threats brought on by unexpected events and lack of sound planning. Even those who seem successful deal with financial issues. Regardless of where you are financially today, the strategies discussed in this book can help you prepare for your retirement years.

The Middle-Class Challenge

Many measures of financial security for the middle class are now in decline. For decades, stagnant wages have been a problem in the United States. The last calendar decade saw two major stock market corrections, and the S&P 500[3] returned a -9.1% over that ten-year period. In addition, during the 2008 debt crisis, people saw the values of their homes plummet. In some areas, many Americans simply walked away from their mortgages and abandoned their dreams of home ownership. This period was especially painful for the millions of hard-working Americans who thought that building their home equity was a guaranteed way to accumulate wealth.

Consider also the continued weakness in the labor market. While the stated rate of unemployment has recovered from its lows of the 2008 recession, it still affects almost 8 million Americans.[4] When

---

[3] *Lost Decade*. (n.d.). Investopedia. Retrieved from http://www.investopedia.com/terms/l/lost-decade.asp (accessed 2 May 2016).

[4] *Economic news release: employment situation summary.* (n.d.). U.S. Bureau of Labor Statistics, U.S. Department of Labor. Retrieved from http://www.bls.gov/news.release/empsit.nr0.htm (accessed 2 May 2016).

you are unemployed, it is nearly impossible to save; and to make matters worse, you may need to take money *out* of existing savings at the same time. Alongside unemployment, there's *underemployment*, where people get part-time or interim jobs while actively searching for full-time, permanent employment. As of May 2016, the U.S. combined unemployment and underemployment rate was 13.7%.[5] The underemployed typically have lower wages and an inability to cover unexpected events. This makes the underemployed particularly vulnerable to slipping out of middle class, at least from the standpoint of being able to afford a home and other necessities. As a person's period of underemployment lengthens, so does his or her probability of being able to save and gain financial freedom at some point in the future.

While underemployment is a challenge across the board, younger Millennials are having an especially difficult time gaining employment that matches their education level. In 2011, more than half of America's recent college graduates were either unemployed or working in a job that didn't require a bachelor's degree, according to the *Associated Press*. More than half (53.6% or 1.5 million people) of bachelor's degree-holders under the age of 25 were jobless or underemployed—that's the highest share since 2000, when the share was at a low of 41%.[6] Regardless of your education, the wake of the Great Recession has been a terrible time to be young and hunting for work.

---

[5] *U.S. underemployment rate from May 2015 to May 2016 (by month)*. (n.d.). Statista. Retrieved from http://www.statista.com/statistics/205240/us-underemployment-rate/ (accessed 26 January 2016).

[6] Weisman, Jordan. (23 April 2012). *53% of recent college grads are jobless or underemployed—how?* The Atlantic. Retrieved from http://www.theatlantic.com/business/archive/2012/04/53-of-recent-college-grads-are-jobless-or-underemployed-how/256237/

Clearly, things are getting tougher for many Americans who are aspiring to achieve financial independence. To help address these challenges, I will share principles and strategies that apply to just about any income level. These practices will work for recent college graduates, self-employed entrepreneurs, blue-collar workers, white-collar executives, and small-business CEOs who aspire to be free from financial worries, as well as the upper-middle class or even the wealthy who already enjoy a sense of financial freedom. You may be in your 20s or 30s and just starting out, or in your 40s or 50s in your peak earning years. Regardless of where you are on the income spectrum, the principles for gaining, maintaining, and managing wealth are similar. And as we will see, the sooner you start the better chance you have to reach your goals.

It is imperative to understand the impact of inflation and the role a sustainable withdrawal rate plays in retirement. Without understanding these concepts, it will be difficult to identify how much money you need to accumulate to meet your retirement savings challenge.

> It is imperative to understand the impact of inflation and the role a sustainable withdrawal rate plays in retirement.

I work with clients regularly who ask me for help in planning their financial futures. They want to know how much it will take to attain financial freedom, without worrying about money or cramping their current spending, and what steps they have to take now to better ensure their financial future. Applying the concepts in this book can help you prepare for a sound financial future.

In this book, I will share with you:

1. Why being a millionaire may not be enough
2. The middle-class outlook

3. How to determine *What Is Your Unique Formula?*™ for your financial freedom
4. Four economic hurdles facing the middle class
5. Four common mistakes that can throw off your financial plan
6. Four enemies of your investment portfolio
7. Financial devastation of the three Ds: death, disability, and divorce
8. Potential shortcomings of your 401(k) plan
9. Your *Countdown to Financial Freedom*
10. My hopes for what's next

You'll find the concepts in this book to be relevant, whether you currently make $50,000 or $500,000. As we saw earlier, most middle-class and affluent people who want to continue to maintain their comfortable lifestyle will need a minimum of $1 million if they are close to retirement age, and considerably more if they are younger.

Your first step in this process will be to make a commitment to your financial success. Self-funding financial independence is no easy task, but it can be done! Once you make the commitment and set your goals, you will also need discipline to stay on track. Without developing a financial savings discipline, the strategies, resources, and tools I suggest will not be very effective. It all starts by taking the time to go through this book, creating a spending plan, and investing with the goals of your written financial plan in mind. With the right goals, plan, and practices, you *can* do it! You can realize your vision of financial freedom, be able to retire when you want, and enjoy life on your terms. I believe this because I've seen many people follow these principles of wise financial planning and enjoy a lifestyle free from financial worries.

CHAPTER 2

The Middle-Class Challenge

If you get a little confused about who exactly is the "middle class," then you are not alone. The concept of middle class can be tricky to talk about, so let's take a moment to define it. First, the middle class is the broad socioeconomic group of people in contemporary society who fall between the working-class and upper-class communities. There are several ways of looking at "middle class:" one is culturally and another is economically (or financially).

Culturally, people identify the middle class by measures such as education level, job type, social strata of one's upbringing, and location of one's home. Other factors can include personal and family values, manners, social norms, and social networks. Many Americans consider themselves to be middle class because they are content or may be happy in how they are living life, regardless of what kind of income they make.

From an economic or financial standpoint, however, middle class can be determined by how your household income compares to your state's median household income. If your household falls within a certain range below or above the median, then you are you are making a middle-class income. We'll talk more about this in the next section of this chapter.

Reporters, analysts, and the general public often fail to identify the specific measure (cultural or financial) when talking about "the middle class" or "middle-class households," and sometimes they're talking about a mix of both measures. So, look to the context of the conversation to get clarity.

A Brush with "Middle-Class Poverty"

Speaking of clarity, let me add some to the term "Middle-Class Poverty." There are clear and cogent differences between federally defined poverty and what I refer to as "Middle-Class Poverty." By no means am I intending to equate the two or diminish the serious problem of federally defined poverty in America. That kind of real poverty is a condition that I am not attempting to address in this book. I am, however, familiar with what it is like to live near that poverty line and face financial hardship. Until age 16, I lived a very modest, middle-class lifestyle in Fort Lee, New Jersey. Then my parents separated, thrusting me, my mother, and my two teenage brothers into a state of financial shock. In the late 1970s, the divorce process was far less fair to women than it is today, and the courts showed little concern for my mother's immediate need to provide for her three children. The four of us had to leave our single-family home and move into a low-rent, one-bedroom apartment in a low-income neighborhood. My mother had had no assets and no income. There was no child support, and there was never any alimony for my mother, even though she had been married and not working outside the home for 20 years.

To gain marketable employment skills, my mother enrolled in a federally sponsored jobs-training program. Meanwhile, my older brother and I used the income from our part-time food-service jobs to pay the rent and buy groceries. In time, she took on an entry-level, administrative position at a local bank and wound up enjoying her work and building her own career. But those first few years were indeed a challenge.

This journey helped me be sensitive to the situation of many American families who are far worse off than my family ever was. I gained a glimpse of what it's like not to be able to afford daily necessities and to have finances factor into just about every decision every day. In a virtual instant, my family went from a solid middle-class life to one filled with the daily concerns of how we would afford food, housing, and college. I knew then that I never again wanted to face that sort of financial anxiety.

This book is about having the lifestyle that you want, including through your retirement years. With the term "Middle-Class Poverty," I'm referring to the condition where you maintain aspects of the middle class, but you can no longer financially afford your desired lifestyle. I want to be your advocate and assist you in your pursuit of your own version of personal financial freedom. When a client asks, "How much money do I need?" there is no one answer; the formula is different based on each person's situation and dreams for their future.

What Is a Middle-Class Income?

As I mentioned above, middle-class income can be determined by how your household income compares to your state's median household income. While there is no universally accepted guideline, a widely respected Pew Charitable Trusts study in 2015 described middle-class households as those making between 67% and 200% of their state's median income.[7] And looking at those numbers across

---

[7] Luhby, Tami. (24 March 2015). *The middle class is getting smaller.* CNN. Retrieved from http://money.cnn.com/2015/03/24/news/economy/middle-class-smaller/

states, the concerning news is that the middle class appears to be shrinking.

Applying the Pew formula to 2013/14 U.S. Census Bureau data, middle-class annual income ranges from $25,309 at the low end in Mississippi to $144,966 at the high end in Maryland. Take a look at Table B. Does your household income fall within the bounds of middle-class income in your state? How does your household compare to your state's median income?

Table B. What You Need to Earn to Be in the Middle Class

STATE	MEDIAN HOUSEHOLD INCOME	MIDDLE CLASS LOWER BOUND	MIDDLE CLASS UPPER BOUND
Maryland	$ 72,483	$ 48,322	$ 144,966
Alaska	$ 72,237	$ 48,158	$ 144,474
New Jersey	$ 70,165	$ 46,777	$ 140,330
Hawaii	$ 68,020	$ 45,347	$ 136,040
District of Columbia	$ 67,572	$ 45,048	$ 135,144
Connecticut	$ 67,098	$ 44,732	$ 134,196
Massachusetts	$ 66,768	$ 44,512	$ 133,536
New Hampshire	$ 64,230	$ 42,820	$ 128,460
Virginia	$ 62,666	$ 41,777	$ 125,332
Minnesota	$ 60,702	$ 40,468	$ 121,404
California	$ 60,190	$ 40,127	$ 120,380
U t ah	$ 59,770	$ 39,847	$ 119,540
Colorado	$ 58,823	$ 39,215	$ 117,646
Wyoming	$ 58,752	$ 39,168	$ 117,504
Washington	$ 58,405	$ 38,937	$ 116,810
Delaware	$ 57,846	$ 38,564	$ 115,692
New York	$ 57,369	$ 38,246	$ 114,738
Illinois	$ 56,210	$ 37,473	$ 112,420
Rhode Island	$ 55,902	$ 37,268	$ 111,804
North Dakota	$ 55,759	$ 37,173	$ 111,518
Vermont	$ 52,578	$ 35,052	$ 105,156
Iowa	$ 52,229	$ 34,819	$ 104,458
Pennsylvania	$ 52,007	$ 34,671	$ 104,014

STATE	MEDIAN HOUSEHOLD INCOME	MIDDLE CLASS LOWER BOUND	MIDDLE CLASS UPPER BOUND
Texas	$ 51,704	$ 34,469	$ 103,408
Wisconsin	$ 51,467	$ 34,311	$ 102,934
Nebraska	$ 51,440	$ 34,293	$ 102,880
Nevada	$ 51,230	$ 34,153	$ 102,460
Kansas	$ 50,972	$ 33,981	$ 101,944
Oregon	$ 50,251	$ 33,501	$ 100,502
South Dakota	$ 48,947	$ 32,631	$ 97,894
Arizona	$ 48,510	$ 32,340	$ 97,020
Michigan	$ 48,273	$ 32,182	$ 96,546
Ohio	$ 48,081	$ 32,054	$ 96,162
Georgia	$ 47,829	$ 31,886	$ 95,658
Indiana	$ 47,529	$ 31,686	$ 95,058
Maine	$ 46,974	$ 31,316	$ 93,948
Montana	$ 46,972	$ 31,315	$ 93,944
Missouri	$ 46,931	$ 31,287	$ 93,862
Idaho	$ 46,783	$ 31,189	$ 93,566
Florida	$ 46,036	$ 30,691	$ 92,072
North Carolina	$ 45,906	$ 30,604	$ 91,812
Oklahoma	$ 45,690	$ 30,460	$ 91,380
Tennessee	$ 44,297	$ 29,531	$ 88,594
Louisiana	$ 44,164	$ 29,443	$ 88,328
South Carolina	$ 44,163	$ 29,442	$ 88,326
New Mexico	$ 43,872	$ 29,248	$ 87,744
Kentucky	$ 43,399	$ 28,933	$ 86,798

STATE	MEDIAN HOUSEHOLD INCOME	MIDDLE CLASS LOWER BOUND	MIDDLE CLASS UPPER BOUND
Alabama	$ 42,849	$ 28,566	$ 85,698
West Virginia	$ 41,253	$ 27,502	$ 82,506
Arkansas	$ 40,511	$ 27,007	$ 81,022
Mississippi	$ 37,963	$ 25,309	$ 75,926

SOURCE: Pew Data and *Business Insider*.[8]

The wide range of middle-class income levels can add to the confusion when talking about the middle class. And there can be a wide range of lifestyle differences depending on where you fall in that income range. If we look at home values as an indicator of lifestyle, the variance is also great. For instance, in two Maryland cities that are both perceived to be desirable middle-class communities, home prices can vary significantly. In Rockville, the median home value is $460,300,[9] while in Frederick, just 30 miles away, the median home value is $251,300.[10] This is a huge difference for cities whose residents often work side by side in the same employment centers. Similarly, consider

> If we look at home values as an indicator of lifestyle, the variance is great.

---

[8] Kane, Libby & Andy Kiersz. (2 April 2015). *How much you have to earn to be considered middle-class in every U.S. state*. Business Insider. Retrieved from http://www.businessinsider.com/middle-class-in-every-us-state-2015-4

[9] *Rockville home prices and values*. (n.d.). Zillow. Retrieved from http://www.zillow.com/rockville-md/home-values/ (accessed 2 May 2016).

[10] *Frederick home prices and values*. (n.d.). Zillow. Retrieved from http://www.zillow.com/frederick-md/home-values/ (accessed 2 May 2016).

Lincolnshire, Illinois, where the median cost of a home is $430,800.[11] Compare that to Cary, less than 23 miles away, where home values average at $210,800.[12] Surely there are differences between these two towns, but the makeup of each is predominantly perceived as middle class.

A 2015 Pew Research Center survey asked families making greater than $100,000 if they felt they were middle class. Given that $100,000 is a lot of money for most Americans, the answers to the Pew survey were surprising. More than half (51%) of those with annual family incomes of $100,000 or more said they belong in the middle class—not the upper class![13]

This is understandable, especially in major urban areas where the costs of living are higher. For example, in Boston, San Francisco, or upscale Manhattan suburbs, a family of four living on a $100,000 income may barely be able to make ends meet. In these urban areas, families need significantly more than a $100,000 per year to feel middle class. Take, for example, a young couple I know that live and work in the heart of Manhattan and earn a combined annual income of $300,000. After paying taxes, and with the expense of two children, they feel like they're barely able to afford the exorbitant rent on their two-bedroom apartment. They have not lived extravagantly, they make good incomes, and yet they have not been able to save for college for their two daughters—they joke that they are hoping for

---

[11] *Lincolnshire home prices and values.* (n.d.). Zillow. Retrieved from http://www.zillow.com/lincolnshire-il/home-values/ (accessed 2 May 2016).

[12] *Cary home prices and values.* (n.d.). Zillow. Retrieved from http://www.zillow.com/cary-il/home-values/ (accessed 2 May 2016).

[13] *Doubts about security of U.S. economic system.* (4 March 2015). Pew Research Center. Retrieved from http://www.people-press.org/2015/03/04/most-say-government-policies-since-recession-have-done-little-to-help-middle-class-poor/doubts-about-security-of-u-s-economic-system/

academic or sports scholarships. They consider themselves barely middle class, and yet their income is considered very high. And according to politicians, they are even "wealthy." When the tax-the-rich argument was raised during the passing of the Patient Protection and Affordable Care Act, additional taxes were established for couples making over $250,000, regardless of whether or not they had any net worth and regardless of the cost of living where they live. While $250,000 could make you quite well-to-do in a rural American town, it doesn't go as far in pricey urban areas.

While happiness is not defined by lifestyle or level of income, there is no question that having more financial resources can help you hurdle life's challenges and feel more secure. Not only will you be more prepared for unexpected costs, like medical bills and home repairs, but you may also have more flexibility to do things that are meaningful to you—like living in your desired neighborhood, sending your kids to good schools, and having a schedule that allows you to be more spontaneous, spend more time with friends and family, and engage in your favorite hobby or charitable cause. Hopefully, the principles and strategies in this book will help you achieve that level of freedom.

Why the Strength of the Middle Class Matters

The American economy cannot seem to shake its unfortunate reality: middle-class people are struggling increasingly to maintain their lifestyle. More than ever, people are talking to me about their fears of having to give up their hard-earned lifestyle, losing their nest eggs, and even being broke. And this middle class concern is not imagined. From 2000 to 2013 the number of middle-class households shrank in all 50 states.[14] Real median household income (income that takes into account inflation over time), according to the 2013 census, is no higher than it was 25 years ago. Put another way, real average hourly wages have barely nudged forward over decades. In fact, in the last 50 years, in real terms, average hourly wages have increased only from $19.18 to $20.67 per hour.[15] With family incomes declining over the last 40 years, the middle class is shrinking: from 61% of all Americans in 1971 to 50% in 2015.[16]

So why does all of this matter? From a societal standpoint, the implications are huge. There will be a potentially massive shift in the way millions of people live once they realize they are grossly underprepared and unable to maintain their current lifestyle. Many people will relocate to less costly areas of the country, cohabitate with friends or relatives, or live meager lifestyles they never imagined. Covering all the cultural and socioeconomic implications is beyond the scope of this book. My emphasis is on empowering you so you don't have to face an unwanted drop in lifestyle. I will focus on increasing your awareness and helping you build better habits to navigate through the financial headwinds you may face on your journey to financial freedom.

---

[14] Desilver, Drew. (14 December 2015). *America's middle class is shrinking: so who's leaving it?* Pew Research Center. Retrieved from http://www.pewresearch.org/fact-tank/2015/12/14/americas-middle-class-is-shrinking-so-whos-leaving-it/

[15] *Federal minimum wage rates 1955–2014.* (n.d.). InfoPlease. Retrieved from http://www.infoplease.com/ipa/A0774473.html (accessed 4 September 2015).

[16] *Are you in the middle class?* (11 May 2016). Pew Research Center. Retrieved from http://www.pewsocialtrends.org/2015/12/09/are-you-in-the-american-middle-class/

Basic Steps and Protections

Wherever they are on the middle-class spectrum, Americans have lifestyle expectations: a certain type of home, a luxury car or SUV, extracurricular activities, a great education for their kids, vacations, and leisure pursuits. Yet when an emergency expense pops up—health care, home repairs, car replacement—the budget is often so tight that other regular expenses have to be deferred until the next pay period. One recent study found that 62% of Americans are unprepared to meet such a financial obligation when it occurs.[17] This failure to prepare for the unexpected can begin a downward spiral from which it is difficult to rebound.

Money magazine estimates that 78% of us will have a major negative financial event in any given 10-year period. A Gallup poll found that only about 4 in 10 Americans say they actually have cash on hand for the inevitable rainy day.[18] In fact, most people said they will rely on other sources of emergency funds, if needed, during a crisis, including credit cards, loans or cash gifts from family members, or 401(k) loans.[19]

Most people would prefer to have liquidity or cash available, for example, in a bank account. Having this "rainy day fund" helps people to worry less about money. Wouldn't it be comforting to know

> Why create and stick to a financial plan as early in life as possible when spending can be more fun?

---

[17] Fottrell, Quetin. (31 January 2015). *Most Americans are one paycheck away from the street*. MarketWatch. Retrieved from http://www.marketwatch.com/story/most-americans-are-one-paycheck-away-from-the-street-2015-01-07

[18] Jacobe, Dennis. (2 June 2005). *Many consumers lack a rainy day fund*. Gallup. Retrieved from http://www.gallup.com/poll/16564/many-consumers-lack-rainy-day-fund.aspx

[19] Ibid.

that an unexpected event will not force you to change your lifestyle? This is a goal most people share, but it is not easy for everyone to achieve. The discipline to create a financial plan and stick to a spending-and-saving plan as early in life as possible is an elusive goal for many. Let's face it, immediate gratification is way more fun! And unfortunately, many of us aren't willing to delay our present wants for our future needs. After all, we're working so hard all the time; don't we deserve to have what we want, when we want it? Enter one of the core challenges of the middle class: saying no to spending today in order to gain financial freedom tomorrow.

While some people don't save money because they choose to spend and consume at will, others aren't saving because they cannot make enough income in today's tight job market. They save what they can, but it's just not enough to cover unexpected expenses. They work second jobs, stay in their careers longer, and face stagnant wages year after year. Weakness in the labor market continues and is evident by factors like the historically low interest rates that have appeared since the economic collapse of 2008. The Federal Reserve Bank (the Fed) continues to cite weakness in the labor market[20] as justification for low interest rates. The economic theory holds that low interest rates can stimulate the job market and the economy. However, after years of a low or no interest rate policy by the Fed, weakness in the labor markets persists.

Just a Crisis Away

It is true that millions of Americans are just one unexpected event away from financial difficulties. Even the comparatively wealthy are

---

[20] Bernanke, Ben. (30 March 2015). *Why are interest rates so low?* Brookings. Retrieved from http://www.brookings.edu/blogs/ben-bernanke/posts/2015/03/30-why-interest-rates-so-low

not immune: one fourth of households making at least $100,000 occasionally live paycheck to paycheck.[21] And job security and a guarantee your career will continue to flourish later in life are far from certain.

You may assume that you're going to work for decades with no interruptions, but as soon as an unplanned event comes along, your financial security can be jeopardized. Here are five crisis events that can derail your financial security:

- Death of a spouse
- Divorce
- Disability
- Health crisis
- Unexpected job loss

We'll discuss these in detail later in the book, but let's look at one example now: divorce. Divorce can be particularly bad news for your financial health for three reasons. First: legal bills are expensive. Second: the splitting of assets, by definition, decreases each party's net worth. Third: the divorce process can be so distressing that people often end up feeling overwhelmed and even debilitated; in such an emotional state, the tendency for making irrational decisions increases at the same time that so many financial issues hang in the balance. I'm not a therapist, but I have worked with both men and women for whom the divorce process was traumatizing and brought on a variety of difficult personal challenges. It is usually a

---

[21] Picchi, Aimee. (17 April 2015). *Earning $75,000 and living paycheck to paycheck.* CBS MoneyWatch. Retrieved from http://www.cbsnews.com/news/earning-75000-and-living-paycheck-to-paycheck/

very difficult time to be making important financial decisions that impact your long-term goals.

I remember one poignant example involving a woman I'll call Tiffany. Tiffany thought she was rich when she received $1.5 million in a divorce settlement. At a sustainable withdrawal rate of 4% per year, the $1.5 million could have provided Tiffany about $60,000 in first-year income. However, Tiffany, like many who grew up during the Batman era, thought that having more than a million dollars meant that she had financial freedom. She wasn't living an exorbitant lifestyle, but she liked nice things, had hobbies that cost some money, and paid for her children's various activities that neither she nor the kids wanted to forego. Tiffany was emotionally attached to a lifestyle that she could no longer afford. She was spending nearly $120,000 per year, about double the $60,000 that would have been sustainable. She was rapidly spending down her principal each month, and given her age (early 50s), Tiffany was on pace to run out of money if she lived a long life

The truth was, unless she lived on less than $60,000 per year, got a reasonably good paying job to supplement her income, or remarried a very wealthy person, she was going to run out of money in her 60s or 70s. And if that happened, she could be left to live solely on social security. Unfortunately, even after hearing these dire predictions, Tiffany continued to cannibalize her principle. It was a case of middle-class poverty waiting to happen. She lived an upper-middle-class lifestyle, but was not willing to change her spending pace to maintain even a middle-class lifestyle. Tiffany is not unlike millions of people in similar circumstances—unwilling to look at the full picture of what might happen if they don't take steps to address their financial situation while they can.

Discipline Pays Off: An Inspiring Story

Not all stories are doom and gloom. Over the past decades, I have watched Matt, a friend of mine from college who came from modest financial roots, reach his financial goals. He had the benefit of sound financial guidance from his parents who often shared their memories of the Great Depression. He also went to an in-state university and did not accumulate large amounts of student debt. And while there, he had a career-based major that he was able to quickly parlay into gainful employment. His parents taught him not to value "keeping up with the Joneses," so he never gave in to the pressure of buying everything that his friends had. Matt didn't make a six-figure income until he was in his late 30s, and he and his wife have never made more than $200,000 in a year, but they faithfully saved a portion of each paycheck.

Although he had the means, Matt would consistently forego the trappings of what appears to be middle-class wealth and opt for a more modest approach. I have seen him buy previously owned, non-luxury cars instead of newer, fancier models. He routinely shopped at the end of the season for his wardrobe to get better prices, and on vacations, he and his family enjoyed staying at comfortable, mid-price hotels versus high-end resorts. Along the way, Matt never felt like he was "missing out" on anything; he always enjoyed the present while also achieving his long-term goals.

Today, in his early 50s, Matt has reached his goals for financial freedom. He chooses to work because he wants to—not because he has to. And while he and his wife can afford private schools, they instead choose to send their two sons to the local public schools. They own a lovely home in a desirable area of New Jersey and comfortably afford family vacations each year. College funds have been set aside, and they live with confidence that they will not run out of money during retirement.

Matt is now a multimillionaire with more financial flexibility than most of the people we knew from our college years. While there is no one-size-fits-all approach, Matt's strategies are tried and true, and they have worked for countless others. If you keep your eye on the ball like Matt did, then you, too, could have the financial confidence to live the life you want.

Pensions Are Great If You Have One

Many government workers and a declining number of private-sector employees—18%, down from 35% in the 1990s[22]—retire with pension plans. For these people, pensions have become a source of wealth. For example, if you were fortunate enough to be working for the state of Nevada, you might be receiving an annual pension of $64,000 during retirement.[23] If your spouse also worked for the state government, your household income, in this theoretical example, would be over $120,000 per year. In contrast, someone who is self-funding, versus receiving a pension, would have to accumulate a $3 million portfolio in order to generate that same $120,000 yearly

---

[22] Morrissey, Monique. (11 January 2013). *Private sector pension coverage fell by half over two decades.* Economic Policy Institute. Retrieved from http://www.epi.org/blog/private-sector-pension-coverage-decline/

[23] Biggs, Andrew G. (March 2014) *Not so modest: Pension benefits for full-career state government employees.* Economic Perspectives. American Enterprise Institute. Retrieved from http://www.aei.org/wp-content/uploads/2014/03/-aei-economic-perspective-march-2014_160053300510.pdf

income (using the 4% sustainable withdrawal rate I explained earlier).[24,25] Therefore, it's easy to see why pensions are highly coveted.

Pensions, especially ones from a strong state or local government, or a very strong corporation, are the gold standard in financial security, but they're becoming scarce. Funding a pension and retirement benefit structure nowadays is a far different matter for employers than it was 25 or 35 years ago. This is largely due to the longer life expectancies enjoyed by Americans.[26] Paradoxically, these longer life expectancies make the need for pensions even greater for our workers and our society; yet at the same time, these longer life expectancies make pensions too costly for many employers who now have to be able to fund the pensions for the additional years that people are living. Hence, private sector pensions are disappearing. Even though this change has come about slowly, over a period of decades, most Americans are still not prepared.

The bottom line is this: if you don't have a pension, you're going to need to self-fund your retirement to supplement whatever social security benefits you get. Self-funded retirement is riskier and more difficult than having a secure pension. To self-fund your future non-working years, you may need to start with substantial principal in order to avoid running out of money later in life. To get that principal, it's important to start saving as early as possible. Even if you have a pension, it's risky to

---

[24] Pfau, Wade. (10 June 2015). *Safe withdrawal rates for retirement and the Trinity Study.* Forbes. Retrieved from http://www.forbes.com/sites/wadepfau/2015/06/10/safe-withdrawal-rates-for-retirement-and-the-trinity-study/

[25] Jaconetti, Colleen M. & Maria A. Bruno. (n.d.). *Spending from a portfolio: Implications of withdrawal order for taxable investors.* Vanguard Investment Counseling & Research, Retrieved from http://www.vanguard.com/pdf/icrsp.pdf (accessed 22 June 2016)

[26] *Calculators: Life expectancy.* (n.d.). U.S. Social Security Administration. Retrieved from https://www.ssa.gov/planners/lifeexpectancy.html (accessed 22 June 2016).

count on it always being there. Political and economic pressures could mean that some pensions may be reduced or go away entirely.

Go Get a Pension

States like Illinois, New York, New Jersey, California, and others have made generous pension promises to their workers. State employees certainly deserve what they've been promised. Our teachers and first responders are the backbone of our communities and deserve their hard-earned pensions. Yet many states are finding the burden of their pension promises too heavy to bear. If the states cannot maintain stable, healthy finances, they may be forced to initiate cutbacks in some important programs. So, the discussion on pensions is very difficult and full of tradeoffs. When these future pension promises were made several decades ago, states did not adequately forecast the true liabilities, nor did they foresee the crunch on taxpayers. With people living longer, it takes increasingly more taxpayer money to keep pensions funded. And as this cost to taxpayers rises, funding all these pension promises has unfortunately become a topic of debate, especially in light of how few Americans are able to adequately fund their own retirements. With state revenues declining in this stagnant national economy, the problem is even more compounded, and to be sure, states will be looking at this closely in the coming decades.

The pension concern can be seen on the local level too. Cities like Detroit, Chicago, and Providence, Rhode Island, are struggling to meet their pension obligations. Local municipalities are not highly diversified in their revenue sources. So when they experience a decline in local population, they have serious financial setbacks that often push their budgets beyond repair. For the city of Detroit, that has meant filing bankruptcy, and in Chicago, the mayor has had to make very tough decisions that have caused tension with the local teachers' union. Rhode Island residents are paying higher taxes to help fund government budgets and employee entitlements such as pensions; yet many of those same residents can't afford to set aside funds for their own retirements. This unexpected pension pressure is bubbling up in state and local municipalities across our country. And it's happening as well at some private companies who have found it too great a burden to honor their hefty pension obligations. Some of these companies are even defaulting on their promises and their benefits.[27]

So, if you have a stable source of hard-earned pension income, consider yourself luckier—and wealthier—than many of your fellow Americans. And if you are well behind on your savings goal, maybe it's wise for you to look for a job that has a generous pension plan, and hope they don't change the terms while you are working there. There are typically vesting periods and other requirements to qualify for pension benefits, so make your decision wisely.

One other note: while pensions are desirable for the income they provide, there is no lump-sum component; you have to receive it in monthly payments. Although you may be receiving a pension and social security payments, you might not have enough cash flow for an occasional indulgence or for an emergency event. Therefore, the principles and advice in this book can apply to you even if you are one of the lucky few with a pension.

Retirement Isn't Cheap

This book focuses on retirement for a big reason: the impoverishment of the middle class often occurs *during* retirement,

---

[27] Brandon, Emily. (23 August 2010). *The 10 biggest failed pension plans.* U.S. News & World Report. Retrieved from http://money.usnews.com/money/blogs/planning-to-retire/2010/08/23/the-10-biggest-failed-pension-plans

when a household's income is no longer provided by earned income and is replaced with income generated by retirement savings, social security, and pensions. When there is inadequate savings, too often what was once a healthy annual income can be slashed by one-third or more. But don't despair! The tools and suggestions in this book can help you pursue your desired lifestyle, despite the hazards of these economic challenges. A lot of people I talk with think that they'll live simpler lives in retirement and just won't need much income. But when I listen to my clients who are already in retirement, I learn that, as you get older, your cost of living doesn't always decline. Yes, some expenses do go away, but new ones creep up. For instance, your house might be paid off, but like you, it is aging. You may want to paint and update the interior or refresh the landscaping. You may need to rehab the siding and gutters, replace the driveway, fix old plumbing, replace the furnace, and so forth. And as you and your house age, you'll need more hired help around the house.

Health care is another expense that usually increases with age. Fewer than 13% of Americans aged 60 or older are *not* on any kind of medication.[28] If you're one of the 87% who *is* on medication, then you're looking at paying for medication and the costs of the associated health issues during your last five-or-so working years, when you might need to be saving for retirement. According to AARP, people who are age 50 or older take, on average, four prescription drugs, while some take ten or more medications. Add a serious illness, like diabetes, cancer, or heart problems, and the costs can reach into the thousands of dollars per month for medication and treatments. The AARP's report on prescription drug use among middle-aged

---

[28] *Prescription drug use continues to increase: U.S. prescription data from 2007–2008.* (n.d.). National Center for Health Statistics, CDC. Retrieved from http://www.cdc.gov/nchs/data/databriefs/db42.htm (accessed 22 June 2016).

and older Americans says the number of medications is increasing. Between 1986 and 2002, Americans age 45 and older reported their regular use of prescription drugs increased from 52% to 75%.[29]

Many retirees enjoy starting new hobbies, traveling to see their children, and spoiling their grandkids. But if you're not financially ready, the expenses associated with these joyful parts of life can contribute to the anxiety of growing older. The nagging doubt that comes with having to constantly worry about what you can afford can rob you of your joy. This is probably not what you want this stage of your life to be about, and it's most certainly not why you worked so hard for so many years.

The Magnitude of the Challenge

As a financial planner, I help people understand whether the reality of their financial present is on track to meet the dreams of their financial future. We have talked in this chapter about some of the unexpected events that can throw people off track, like job loss, family crises, and so on. As we work together to address these issues, I often have the pleasure of seeing my clients, though some reluctantly, begin to prepare for such unexpected events and move closer to reaching their goals and dreams. When you're young and just starting out, the best way to advance your financial goals and dreams is to automatically save a portion of your income from each paycheck. Again and again in my career, I have seen people save their way to financial freedom, many of whom who started with nothing in the bank, no pension, and no inheritance. They have come from a variety of backgrounds, but there's one thing they all have had in common:

---

[29] Barrett, Ph.D., Linda, L. (January 2005). *Prescription drug use among midlife and older Americans.* AARP. Retrieved from http://assets.aarp.org/rgcenter/health/rx_midlife_plus.pdf

they never wavered in their conviction that saving now is worth the payoff later.

> When you hear someone say you need a million (current) dollars saved to retire, generally that amount will yield about $40,000 a year in sustainable cash flow.

If you have a fear or anxiety about the need to plan for retirement, you may put off financial decisions of any kind; it may be easier to do nothing than to face those fears. Part of the fear may be based on the unknown outcomes of your decisions and may require a little faith to overcome. Your anxiety may also come, in part, from not knowing which financial expert opinion to trust regarding the *amount* of money you need to accumulate. Some experts suggest saving 20% of your income, but this depends on when you get started and may assume a lifetime rate of savings with no interruptions.[30] Conventional wisdom suggests between $1 million and $2 million is an appropriate amount for near retirees to have saved in order to maintain a comfortable, middle-class lifestyle. Your specific savings needs will be unique to you. Later, I will share with you a methodology to help determine specifically how much you might need to start saving each month. For now, here's a quick guideline to keep in mind:

When you hear someone say you need a million (current) dollars saved to retire, generally that amount will yield about $40,000 a year in sustainable cash flow. When you hear you need to have $2 million saved, picture yourself living on $80,000 per year (less any impact of future inflation).

The *distribution phase* of life is when you are no longer accumulating assets but rather consuming or spending them. So,

---

[30] Ibid.

in your planning efforts, think in terms of a distribution rate or sustainable withdrawal rate. Instead of thinking, "How much money do I have?" think, "How much cash flow will this money generate for me in the future, and will it be enough to live the life I want?"

A lot of people don't know the numerical magnitude of their retirement shortfall. As I mentioned earlier, conventional wisdom suggests between $1 million and possibly $2 million as an acceptable amount for current and near retirees to have accumulated to remain in the middle class in retirement; yet a majority (60%) of workers in a recent *USA Today* survey indicated they currently have less than $25,000 in their savings accounts.[31] Only 44% reported even looking into what amount they might require.[32] The magnitude of the challenge is vast, but it doesn't have to be insurmountable for you. Take steps to overcome any fears, and trust that your anxieties will diminish as you get into the process. I have clients of all ages who come in with a lot of fear about the challenge ahead, yet they move past those fears as their plans are set into motion.

So What Am I Advocating?

Much like any 10-step program, the first step to financial health is awareness and making a commitment to a achieving a more successful outcome. With awareness, commitment, and proper planning, including a written plan, you can avoid Middle-Class Poverty *and* enjoy the financial life you want. If you want help with your plan, seek out a qualified professional.

---

[31] Hellmich, Nancy. (1 April 2014). *Retirement: A third have less than $1,000 put away.* USA Today. Retrieved from http://www.usatoday.com/story/money/personalfinance/2014/03/18/retirement-confidence-survey-savings/6432241/

[32] Ibid.

Like any other aspect of your life, reaching your financial goals will take focus, effort, and some tradeoffs. In later chapters, we'll discuss some of the traps and headwinds you will face on your financial journey. In chapter 9, I'll talk about the different things you can be doing in each decade of your life to better prepare for retirement. Don't worry if you're in your 40s, 50s, or even 60s. It's never too late to prepare for your retirement or financial freedom.

CHAPTER 3

What Is Your Unique Formula™?

A Formula Focus

It seems like everyone is asking, "What's your number?" From your credit score, to the firmness of your mattress, to your body mass index (BMI), there's a personal number for so many things these days. In the world of financial planning, "your number" usually indicates the estimated amount of assets you need in order to help you reach your financial goals (e.g., funding your retirement). From my perspective, talking about a *number* is not adequate. Instead, I prefer to focus on a complete *formula process* for determining the estimated amount of assets you will need in order to generate your desired amount of retirement income. Retirement means different things for different people, but one thing is fairly consistent: most people would prefer to work only because they *want to* and not because they have to. When the ability to do that is achieved, I call it "financial freedom."

Everyone's formula for calculating their desired retirement income, and the journey they will take to reach it, is unique. That's why I developed a process I call *What Is Your Unique Formula?*™. I feel so strongly about this process, that I had the phrase trademarked.

To determine Your Unique Formula, you'll first need to identify 1) your current retirement assets and savings, 2) your discretionary monthly income available for saving, and 3) a realistic assessment of any inheritances (or gifts); from there, you'll calculate 4) your estimated assets at retirement, and finally 5) your projected retirement income. In Appendix A at the end of this book, you'll find an illustration of these steps and the needed calculations. Let's discuss each of the 5 steps in detail.

Step 1: Determine Your Current Retirement Savings (CRS)

To begin, you need to know your starting point or your current amount of assets you have saved for retirement. Total all your existing investments that can help you pay for your retirement. These assets, which I call your Current Retirement Savings (CRS), will be your foundation on your path to funding your future financial freedom.

Step 2: Determine Your Monthly Savings (MS)

The next step is to calculate how much you can set aside for ongoing savings each month. I call this your "Monthly Savings (MS)." There are four parts to this step:

1. Understand your take-home pay.
2. Total your monthly expenses.
3. Calculate your monthly discretionary income, which is your take home pay minus your monthly expenses.
4. Determine how much you can save each month.

Take-home Pay

Understanding your monthly, after-tax, take-home pay (after outlays such as health insurance premiums) is a crucial part of this process and essential to your cash-flow planning. Your after-tax take home pay is your total income less taxes, cost of your benefits such as health care insurance, and any 401(k) or other retirement plan contributions. If you are contributing to a 401(k) plan or other retirement plan through your employer, include it later in your Monthly Savings calculation.

Monthly Expenses

Next, ask yourself (and your spouse or life partner, if applicable), "How much do I need for essential living expenses and other important expenses?" You should always include whatever is important to each family member, such as vacations, entertainment, wardrobe purchases, home improvements, kids' activities, charitable contributions, personal trainers, trips to the salon, and so on. If you or your family values something, then it needs to be on this list in order for your list of expenses to be accurate. To help with this process, I recommend completing a cash-flow worksheet (a sample is provided at the end of this book in Appendix B), which will prompt you to remember all your recurring and periodic monthly expenses. It's also a good idea to allow for unexpected expenses to develop a more realistic assessment of your potential monthly cash-flow needs.

Monthly Discretionary Income

Next, subtract the amount of your monthly expenses from the amount of your monthly take-home pay. The difference is either a surplus or deficit. Any surplus is your *monthly discretionary income.* To determine your monthly surplus or discretionary income, the fundamental questions are as follows:

> *How much after-tax income do you have available to live on each month?*
> *How much do you need to comfortably live on each month?*
> *How much is left to save?*

Monthly Savings

If you have a monthly surplus, then deciding to save this amount on an automatic basis (before it ever hits your checking account) can be *the single most important thing* you do to advance your financial plan and pursuit of financial freedom. Of course, there are some situations when you might have an irregular income stream, like receiving a bonus or exercising stock grants, but the process is still basically the same. For employees at the executive level of publicly traded corporations, your company may reward you with bonuses or stock grants. If you are fortunate enough to be in this situation, and you may be able to pay for your recurring, required expenses with your recurring monthly income, then consider saving your entire net bonus or after-tax stock grant proceeds. Sure, an occasional splurge is expected and warranted to keep you motivated and reward your hard work, but overall, bonuses and one-time income events are great ways to fund long-term goals like retirement.

On the other hand, there may be a monthly deficit instead of a surplus. If this is the case, then *What Is Your Unique Formula?* is an even more important process because it can help you get on a better track. In either case, completing a cash-flow worksheet to identify your discretionary income can provide a solid beginning step on your financial journey.

If you have surplus cash flow or discretionary income, consider contributing even more to your 401(k), as that money is invested on an automatic basis before your money hits your checking account where it could otherwise be spent. There are many different types of accounts that can also be a good place to start sending this excess cash flow—the real key is to try very hard not to tap into your savings or investment account once the money has been saved.

Step 3: Estimate Any Expected Inheritance (EI)

Identify the timing and total estimated amount of any gifts, inheritances, or other windfalls you're likely to receive. I call this your Estimated Inheritance (EI).

Let's take a minute to discuss the realities of large gifts or inheritances. First, it's important to be realistic. In the back of your mind, if you think a bailout—either by lottery or an enormous inheritance—is in your future, you may be wishful thinking, and that can undermine your financial goals. It's a risky way to approach financial planning, yet a full 10% of Americans fall into this category. They rely on potential inheritances or unearned financial windfalls *entirely* as their source of retirement income[33] (as evidenced by the nearly 50% of workers in the U.S. who are estimated to have current savings of $25,000 or less for retirement[34]). Unfortunately, there is no retirement fairy that will come along and magically reverse a lack of sound financial planning.

All magic fairy dust aside, in many cases an inheritance can be a real possibility. If, within a few years, you are going to inherit a significant amount of money, you can include it in your calculation. But be realistic and consider the circumstances that can erode your

---

[33] Ellis, Blake. (December 2013). *Average American Inheritance: 177,000.* CNN Money. Retrieved from http://money.cnn.com/2013/12/13/retirement/american-inheritance/

[34] Zalinski, Ernie J. (n.d.). *Saving for Retirement.* Retrieved from http://www.retirement-cafe.com/Saving-for-Retirement.html (accessed 22 June 2016).

actual amount. For example, parents and relatives are living longer, which can delay your receipt of any assets. The record for American life expectancy hit an all-time high in 2014.[35] Along with longer life expectancies, there is a real risk of costly, end-of-life care that may gobble up a significant portion of assets designated for you and other heirs.

Take, for example, a study published in the February 2013 issue of *The Journal of General Internal Medicine* and supported in part by the National Institute on Aging. The study examined out-of-pocket household spending on medical care of more than 3,000 participants. The results were startling. On average, people with Medicare coverage still paid $38,688 per year for medical care in the last five years of life.[36]

Twenty-five percent of participants spent an average of $101,791 out-of-pocket for medical services.[37] During the five-year study, 43% incurred total expenses that exceeded their assets, excluding the value of their homes, and 25% of those surveyed incurred out-of-pocket medical expenses that exceeded the total value of their assets. Essentially, this means that end-of-life care wiped out one-out-of-four people's entire net worth. Costs like these can leave a spouse in a difficult financial predicament. And if there are children, the out-of-pocket cost of end-of-life care may eliminate any chance of the

---

[35] Copeland, Larry. (9 October 2014). *Life expectancy in the USA hits a record high*. Retrieved from http://www.usatoday.com/story/news/nation/2014/10/08/us-life-expectancy-hits-record-high/16874039/

[36] McWilliams, MD, PhD. Michael J. (February 2013). *Out-of-pocket medical spending and Charon's Obol*. Retrieved from http://www.ncbi.nlm.nih.gov/pmc/articles/PMC3614123/

[37] Kelley, MD, MSHS, Amy S. (28 February 2013). *Out-of-pocket spending in the last five years of life*. Journal of General Internal Medicine. 2013 Feb; 28(2): 304–309. Published online 2012 September 5. doi: 10.1007/s11606-012-2199-x. Retrieved from http://www.ncbi.nlm.nih.gov/pmc/articles/PMC3614143/

family passing on wealth to the next generation, thereby continuing the cycle of financial struggle.

One of the major goals of the Medicare legislation enacted in 1965 was to protect elderly citizens from this financial risk. As President Lyndon Johnson declared at the signing of the legislation, "No longer will illness crush and destroy the savings that [older Americans] have so carefully put away over a lifetime."[38]

While Johnson's goals may have been admirable, unfortunately, the reality is that even Medicare will not cover all the related costs for care. Families expecting Medicare to cover long-term-care expenses (e.g., nursing home or assisted living) may be shocked to learn that Medicare doesn't cover those costs. Long-term care expenses and home health care expenses are two of the highest out of pocket costs for older Americans.[39] And if you think the recently passed Patient Protection and Affordable Care Act with its 10,000 plus pages of regulations covers these non-acute care, end-of-life situations, think again. Although it attempted to, and despite the good intentions and admirable goals of some legislators, there was just no funding available for such a huge undertaking.[40]

> Medicare will not cover all the related costs for long-term care like nursing homes, assisted living, and home health care.

If illness or home health care doesn't destroy your chance of receiving an inheritance, another threat can come in the form of a

---

[38] Beschloss, M. (2006). *Our documents: 100 milestone documents from the National Archives.* New York, NY. Oxford University Press.

[39] Graham, Judith. (21 September 2012). *The high cost of out-of-pocket expenses.* The New York Times. Retrieved from http://newoldage.blogs.nytimes.com/2012/09/21/the-high-cost-of-out-of-pocket-expenses/

[40] O'Donnell, Jane & Akinnibi, Fola. (25 October 2013). *How many pages of regulations are in the Affordable Care Act?* USA Today. Retrieved from http://www.usatoday.com/story/opinion/2013/10/23/affordable-care-act-pages-long/3174499/

re-marriage of one of your parents. If one of your parents remarries, and the new spouse replaces you in the will, your inheritance can be reduced or eliminated overnight.

Keep in mind, there is always the specter of estate taxes. Estate taxes can further erode your inheritance (although federal estate taxes only kicked in for estates worth more than $5,430,000 in 2016, some states still retain thresholds that allow state-level estate taxes to take effect for lesser amounts).[41] Tax laws, of course, can change between now and the anticipated passing of a family member. So, keep an eye on developments in estate law as part of your planning.

Finally, if there are several other beneficiaries of the estate, or if the estate is disputed and litigated in court, the amount you ultimately receive might not be what you had expected. For reasons like these, you can't always count your prospective inheritance as a certainty.

Step 4: Calculate Estimated Assets at Retirement (EAR)

Once you determine your Current Retirement Savings (CRS), your Monthly Savings (MS), and any Expected Inheritances (EI), you need to determine the *Future Value (FV)* of each of them as of your projected retirement starting date. To do this, estimate a compound *real rate of growth* (your estimated rate of growth minus an expected rate of inflation) for the number of years from now until your target retirement date. You will need a financial calculator, online tools, or the help of a financial advisor. For the full formula and detailed calculations, go to the end of this chapter.

---

[41] *Small business & self employed: Estate taxes* (n.d.). IRS. Retrieved from http://www.irs.gov/Businesses/Small-Businesses-&-Self-Employed/Estate-Tax (accessed 22 June 2016).

For example, if you estimate that you can grow your assets at 5% per year greater than the rate of inflation, have $400,000 in CRS, can maintain a $1,000 MS rate, have a $250,000 EI in ten years, and you are 20 years away from retirement, your Estimated Assets at Retirement (EAR) will be $1,879,576.41.

Step 5: Calculate your Projected Retirement Income

Once you total the future values of these three 'buckets of money' (CRS, MS, and any EI), and you add them together, take this total and multiply it by your Sustainable Withdrawal Rate, as follows:

{Future Value of your Current Retirement Savings (FVCRS), + Future Value of your Monthly Savings (FVMS) + Future Value of any Expected Inheritance (FVEI) = Estimated Assets at Retirement (EAR)} x Sustainable Withdrawal Rate (SWR).

The resulting product is the estimated amount of cash flow you can self-fund at retirement age.[42] Continuing our example, $1,879,576.41 x .04 = $75,183.06 of estimated first year, self-funded retirement income.

To your result, add any Pensions (P), any Social Security Income (SSI), and any other income on which you might be able to rely. The result is an estimated *total* amount of annual cash flow that you can reasonably expect to live on at retirement. In this example, if P is zero and SSI is $20,000 then total first year retirement cash flow is $95,183.06.

---

[42] Your SWR will be specific to your situation, taking into account things like your current age, life expectancy, your asset allocation, and potential rates of return. It is intended to be a guideline not a certainty for everyone.

And remember, since we took the expected real rate of return (your estimated rate of growth less expected inflation) your future estimated cash flow is already adjusted for inflation. When you look at your numbers, hopefully you'll be happy with the result. This is how I like to write Your Unique Formula:

$$\{(FVCRS + FVMS + FVEI) \times SWR\} + P + SSI = ☺$$

Your income estimate will subsequently fluctuate for cost-of-living adjustments in social security income and changes in your investment value; but you can use this income estimate as guidance when estimating how much cash flow you might have at your target age for financial freedom.

Step-by-step Summary

So in review, here is a step-by-step summary of how to answer *What Is Your Unique Formula?*

1. Add all your current assets and grow them at an estimated inflation-adjusted growth rate for the number of years until your target age for financial freedom.
2. Grow your monthly savings by an inflation-adjusted rate of return to estimate their future value.
3. Estimate all expected gifts or inheritances (that you will save and not spend) plus any inflation-adjusted growth from the time you receive them to your retirement age.
4. Add these three different asset amounts.
5. Multiply this total by your Sustainable Withdrawal Rate of 4%.
6. Add your Pensions and Social Security Income.

The result is your estimated cash flow when you retire. Call me hopeful, but I like to use a happy face (☺) in the formula to symbolize the result. If you don't get a happy face with your result, raise the amount of your monthly savings until you get to a result that satisfies you. Then endeavor to save that amount each month on an automatic basis.

Applying the Formula

Here is another hypothetical example:

$900,000 (FVCRS)
+ $900,000 (FVMS)
+ $200,000 (FVEI)
× .04 (SWR) = $80,000
+ $0 pension (P)
+ $25,000 of Social Security Income (SSI)
= $105,000 in the first year of retirement.

If the person in the above hypothetical example is a 65-year-old who is retiring today, that retiree does not have to estimate future asset values. His or her future is here now, which means future values are the same as current values for the purpose of this exercise. In this case there is a total amount of assets of $2,000,000, and multiplying that by a 4% sustainable withdrawal rate, this person generates $80,000 in the first year of retirement, plus any pensions or social security. If this retiree's pension and social security is $25,000 at age 65, he or she can generate an estimated cash flow of $105,000.

However, if we keep everything the same except adjust the age to a 50-year-old, the impact of inflation makes the future retirement values worth less on an inflation-adjusted basis versus today. Using our previous 3% assumed inflation, this 50-year-old, who eventually retires in 15 years with the same $2,000,000 in assets, has the equivalent of only $1,283,724 in today's dollars. Using a 4% sustainable withdrawal rate, this generates year-one retirement cash flow of $51,349 in real terms. This amount is far less than the $80,000 the 65-year-old retiree's $2,000,000 generated using the same assumed 4% withdrawal rate. If we add the same $25,000 of social security income, this 50-year-old will have year-one retirement income in real terms of $76,349. As you can see, this same $2,000,000 for someone who is age 65 today is a worth a lot more than that same $2,000,000 for someone who is working to accumulate that amount in 15 years.

The impact of inflation is even more pronounced for someone who is 40 or younger. For someone who plans to retire in 25 years at age 65 with $2,000,000, their savings will be worth only $955,211 in today's dollars and generate only $38,208 in real annual income. So, a younger person needs even more money to combat the effects of inflation. This is why I use the term "Million-Dollar Poverty," specifically as it addresses the challenge of Millennials and even Gen X-ers. Younger people may have to think in terms of having millions of dollars simply to generate an income that, in real terms, is barely middle class.

> Younger people may have to think in terms of having millions of dollars simply to generate an income that, in real terms, is barely middle class.

Are You on Track?

When you complete Your Unique Formula and look at your result, do you like what you see? *Does it equal or surpass your hoped for amount of retirement income?* If so, then you have a happy face (☺). And that is the goal: personal happiness.

If you are in the fortunate position of having a projected amount of retirement cash flow *greater* than what you need to live on, you may have a higher amount of current income to spend and enjoy now. Alternatively, you can continue to save at your ambitious pace and target a higher amount of desired financial freedom or retirement income; or you may decide to aim for an earlier retirement date. Everyone's formula is different, but it all comes down to basic arithmetic. That's the beauty of *What Is Your Unique Formula?* It gives you a framework to change the variables, see various outcomes, and make decisions about the financial direction you want to take.

If you are behind on your goals, this process eliminates your ability to use a lack of knowledge as an excuse and helps you face any possible denial head-on.

Behind on Your Goals?

What if your result *doesn't* lead to a happy face? If you are not saving enough because your income is too low, then you need to find a way to earn more money or spend less of your current income. If you determine that you cannot reduce spending and that you need to increase your income in order to save, then consider what your options are within your current career. Talk to your employer about your ambitions and possible advancement, network with your peer group about other opportunities, or if you are self-employed, take an objective look at your situation and consider strategies to improve your business. Alternatively, if you feel you are earning your maximum in your chosen profession, then consider supplementing your income with a "hobby job" or part-time work in a field that you enjoy. Then take as much as you can of this extra income (or all of it!) and save it toward your goals. In other words, if having financial freedom is important to you, somehow, you have to save more.

If you're behind on your goals and you are not saving enough, completing the *What is Your Unique Formula?* process may serve as a wake-up call. It's like when a smoker goes to the doctor. He knows he shouldn't be smoking. He had planned to quit someday, but seeing his lung x-ray gets his attention and motivates him to make a change in his life for the better. Similarly, I hope the process of determining *What Is Your Unique Formula?* will be the catalyst for ultimately gaining the financial life that you want.

Why is it important to start now? Each year you wait to work on Your Unique Formula, you lose the potential value of compound interest, and you have less time to save and accumulate for retirement. If you wait, you have to save more each month once you do start working towards your goals. This is a simple mathematical fact, and it underscores the urgency of starting on your plan as soon as possible.

Sounds simple, easy, and logical, but people are rarely able to change their behavior overnight. In fact, of the 45% of Americans who bother to make a New Year's resolution, only 8% of them manage to keep those resolutions, which are typically much easier to accomplish than gaining your financial freedom.[43] But I have seen people use this process as a springboard for change, and you can change, too. Gaining awareness of a situation is a good place to start and can initiate the beginnings of a positive outcome.

If you have difficulty finding the discipline to take these steps, or if numbers just aren't your thing, then working in partnership with a financial planner can have a tremendous impact. You can liken it to paying for a personal fitness trainer. When people begin paying to work

---

[43] Norcross, John C. & Dominic J. Vangarelli. (1989). *The resolution solution: Longitudinal examination of New Year's change attempts.* Journal of Substance Abuse. 1988-1989;1(2):127-34. Retrieved from http://www.ncbi.nlm.nih.gov/pubmed/2980864

out with a trainer, they often decide to put more effort into their fitness regimen. The underlying psychology of making a commitment to your financial fitness works in a similar manner. In this sense, the process you undertake in determining *What Is Your Unique Formula?* is an exercise in your financial fitness. I know it takes a lot of commitment to continuously self-fund your retirement. But once you start seeing the results, you will feel pretty good, which, in turn, will fuel even more commitment. I saw how meaningful and beneficial making a commitment was long before I started my own financial planning firm.

Examples of Smart Planning

When I was a professor in the University of Maryland system, I became friends with a student of mine named Mike. Mike was a diligent student, always attentive in class, and eager to learn more about finance. He was just starting out as a junior executive at a major defense contractor and finishing the college degree he never had the resources to complete earlier in life. About 15 years later, I bumped into Mike. We sat down together, and he shared his impressive story.

Mike explained how he implemented the basic beginning steps of getting a written financial plan and making regular monthly contributions into an investment account. He also maximized his 401(k) contributions, maintained liquidity, and even bought a house in a popular neighborhood. By the time we had reconnected, Mike had weathered a corporate downsizing and another job change, the 2008 financial crisis, a downturn in home prices, and various personal challenges. Through it all, he remained on track for the lifestyle he wants to enjoy when he reaches his target retirement age of 60. He asked if he should hire me to help him, but I told him he was doing just fine on his own. He had the drive, desire, discipline, and just enough knowledge to do his own planning. When he was recently downsized out of a job again, he called me without an ounce of worry about the layoff. He reduced his expenses, was able to live off his severance package, and avoided dipping into his savings while he looked for another job. Because he had taken the disciplined steps earlier in his life, he was able to deal with this unexpected financial jolt in a manner that allowed him to sleep at night. And that is a goal of this book—to help you have that same freedom from worrying about money.

James Rosseau followed a similar path. James is President, Business Solutions, at LegalShield, headquartered in Oklahoma. Long before James became a successful executive, he and his family lived beneath their means, which, as I mentioned earlier, is often the first step to achieving financial freedom. In an interview for this book, James shared several ways he planned his financial future:

> "Early in my career, we focused on saving and paying down debt. When I got a bonus or any extra money, I tried to put it towards the mortgage and pay down the principal. Even if I've taken out a home equity against it, I've never taken more than I have sitting in cash somewhere. It's not a luxurious house; it's not a big house, but it's ours free and clear."

James also shared that he is very debt averse, which means he doesn't like having a lot of debt and pays with cash whenever possible. Even in starting a new business, he prefers not to depend on other people's money (OPM). He shared that both of those things—owning your own home and not being in debt—give people a stronger sense of personal freedom and control in their lives.

While working at JPMorgan Chase, James said his boss, Lisa, gave him some excellent advice on his third day on the job. "Whatever you do, don't get the golden handcuffs," she said. James asked her, "What do you mean the golden handcuffs?" Lisa explained, "Well, you start getting these bonuses, stock options, and raises, and you start living into them. They become an expected part of your economic life. The people who spend them in advance never get the financial security needed to chart their own course." James was not of this mindset. He said he quickly learned that the more he managed to accumulate (e.g., house, car, savings, investments, and so on), the easier it was to maintain his sense of independence. He pursued his financial freedom with vigor. "I needed to live without the fear of being fired."

James went on to say that the biggest mistake he's seen people make is assuming the next bonus check or paycheck will come indefinitely. People don't plan for the day those checks stop. "That's a fatal flaw," he said. "I've seen so many people get laid off because of decisions a company makes. Some people spend a future bonus that they haven't yet received, thinking they're going to get one every year. And then, if they don't get a bonus, and if they don't have a job, everything comes crashing down." James advises: Be smart about what you spend, and if you're going to use your credit card, pay it all off at the end of the month, so you don't pay interest on it.

In Mike and James, we can see subtle differences in approach, but they have used similar sound financial planning strategies. They planned early, avoided unnecessary debt, built solid liquidity, lived beneath their means, and saved excess cash flow each month or at bonus time. In other words, they set goals and stuck to their financial plan. This commitment and discipline is a key ingredient in personal financial success.

Summary

Once you go through this process and make a commitment to yourself and your future, knowing how to use *What Is Your Unique*

Formula? will help propel you toward the outcome you desire. Here are some key points to remember:

- When you ask yourself, "How much do I need in order to achieve my financial freedom," think of the answer not just as a number, but as a process and a formula.

- Commit to understanding the *What Is Your Unique Formula?* process to see if you are on track to meet your goals.

- Find the time to gather all your personal financial data (e.g., your current assets, take-home pay, monthly savings) and get excited about your journey and the idea of being disciplined.

- Find the resources that will help you calculate Your Unique Formula and develop your written plan for reaching your financial freedom. Review and update your plan yearly.

- Exercise spending discipline in your daily life and enjoy seeing your savings grow as you begin to visualize your financial freedom.

- If you have a shortfall, take corrective action now! It's never too late to positively impact your retirement funding.

- Start today to reduce the chances you have to play a difficult game of catch-up later. Waiting works against you. Waiting reduces the amount of time you are contributing to your goals and reduces the amount of time you can be benefitting from the power of compounding interest.[44]

---

[44] Definition of compound interest: Interest added not only to the principal of a loan or savings account but also to the interest already added to the loan or account.

CHAPTER 4

Four Hurdles on Your Path to Financial Freedom

Four of the major factors threatening the middle-class way of life are (1) stagnant wages and underemployment, (2) increasing health-care costs, (3) an increasing tax burden, and (4) the rising cost of living. This combination of factors has eroded the ability of the middle class to create and maintain a lifestyle comparable to that of previous generations. To combat the impact of these factors on your future lifestyle, it's helpful to take ownership of the challenge ahead. Start by understanding Your Unique Formula for financial success, then plan accordingly and take action. Let's look more deeply at each of these challenges.

Hurdle #1: Stagnant Wages and Underemployment

Based on Federal Reserve data, wages have been climbing only at an average 2.0% pace since the end of 2009, which is considered weak relative to the 50-year historical wage growth average.[45] This

---

[45] *Average hourly earnings of production and nonsupervisory employees: Total private (AHETPI)*. (4 December 2015). Economic Research, Federal Reserve Bank of St. Louis. Retrieved from https://research.stlouisfed.org/fred2/series/AHETPI

recent period of wage stagnation is especially disappointing given the historically low interest rates, increases in productivity, and a monumental stock market rally. For wages not to have significantly increased during a period of economic growth may indicate a deeper, structural problem for workers in a new, rapidly changing economy.

There is a rising school of thought that blames globalization for America's disappointing employment situation.[46] American jobs have been outsourced overseas where there are millions of people standing by to take on work at wage levels substantially lower than their American counterparts. Free trade agreements, like the North American Free Trade Agreement (NAFTA) that took effect in 1994, often take the brunt of the blame, although it is hard to definitively ascertain if this is the case.[47] Other experts point to low-cost Chinese and other overseas manufacturing as a source of pain for U.S. workers.[48] Technology has also been tapped as a cause for worker displacement, and the rapid development and use of technology underscores the need for us to retrain our workforce.[49] Some experts have commented that the slow wage growth can also be attributed to rising regulatory

---

[46] Pompa, Claudi. (March 2015). *Jobs for the future.* ODI Report, Overseas Development Institute. Retrieved from http://www.odi.org/sites/odi.org.uk/files/odi-assets/publications-opinion-files/9578.pdf

[47] Katel, Peter. (22 July 2011). *Reviving manufacturing: Can the U.S. regain its global lead—and factory jobs?* CQ Researcher, vol. 21, issue 26. Retrieved from http://library.cqpress.com/cqresearcher/document.php?id=cqresrre2011072200

[48] *Labor pains.* (2 November 2014). The Economist. Retrieved from http://www.economist.com/news/finance-and-economics/21588900-all-around-world-labour-losing-out-capital-labour-pains

[49] Rottman, David. (12 June 2013). *How technology is destroying jobs.* MIT Technology Review. Retrieved from http://www.technologyreview.com/featuredstory/515926/how-technology-is-destroying-jobs/

changes and costs.[50] In recent years, businesses have faced intense scrutiny, especially in the banking and mortgage sectors. They have been hit with record fines and new regulations. Health care has also experienced significant change, with the full impact of the Patient Protection and Affordable Care Act still unknown. In addition, other old-line industries such as coal are becoming less relevant, and well-paying jobs are disappearing in areas of the country where fewer opportunities exist.[51] And some argue that good old-fashioned corporate greed is also making it difficult for the majority of workers, while the few at the top experience the greatest benefit.

Whatever the reasons for our slow economic recovery and the decline in wage growth, the reality is the decline has been decades in the making and is the result of a variety of factors. Until we reverse this trend, it will be up to people individually to arm themselves with the skills needed to thrive in this new economy; it will be incumbent upon each person to institute a set of personal behaviors that will allow for personal wealth accumulation and financial freedom.

The slowing wage growth is occurring during a period when American workers are keeping up their end of the bargain. Productivity has been increasing at a rate greater than their wage gains. For example, during the Great Recession and its immediate aftermath (i.e., between 2007 and 2012), economy-wide productivity grew 7.7%. Meanwhile, several available measures of wage and compensation growth lagged far behind productivity during this

---

[50] *The rising cost of compliance.* (n.d.). Thomson Reuters. Retrieved from https://risk.thomsonreuters.com/infographic/2015-the-rising-cost-of-compliance (accessed 22 June 2016).

[51] Mishel, Lawrence, Gould, Elise, & Josh Bivens. (6 January 2015). *Wage stagnation in nine charts.* Economic Policy Institute. Retrieved from http://www.epi.org/publication/charting-wage-stagnation/

same period. For example, compensation grew 0.9% as measured by the Labor Productivity and Costs (LPC) program, was flat at 0.0% as measured by the Employment Cost Index (ECI), and fell 0.6% as measured by the Employer Costs for Employee Compensation (ECEC) program.[52]

This trend in slowing wage growth is decades in the making. In Figure A, you can see the average annual growth rate in hourly earnings for private sector, production, and nonsupervisory employees by decade since 1965.[53]

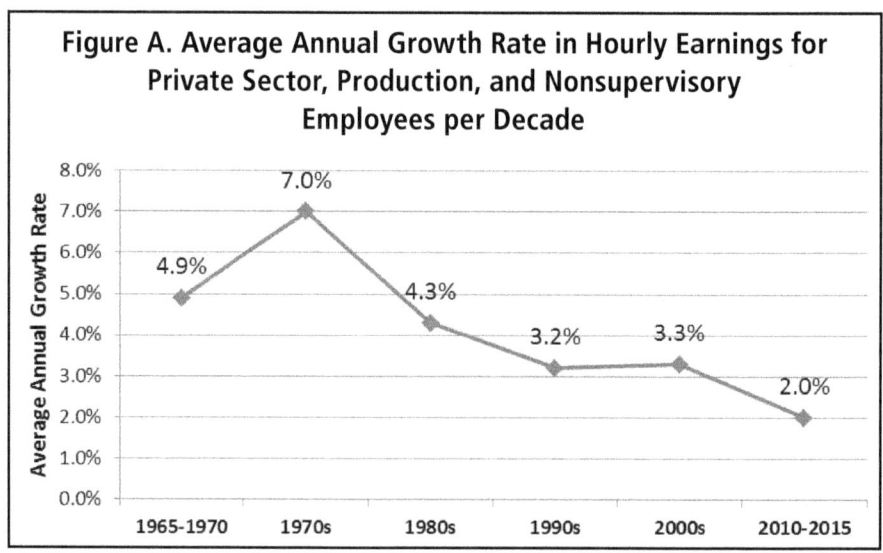

SOURCE: U.S. Bureau of Labor Statistics and Potomac Wealth Advisors, LLC

---

[52] Shierholz, Heidi, & Lawrence Mishel. (21 August 2013). *A decade of flat wages: The key barrier to shared prosperity and a rising middle class*. Economic Policy Institute. Retrieved from http://www.epi.org/publication/a-decade-of-flat-wages-the-key-barrier-to-shared-prosperity-and-a-rising-middle-class/

[53] *Corporate profits after tax: Growth in real private sector wages*. (n.d.). Economic Research: Federal Reserve Bank of St. Louis. Retrieved from https://research.stlouisfed.org/fred2/series/AHETPI (accessed 22 June 2016)

These recent meager gains in wages have also occurred during a stock market rally where the S&P 500 has risen sharply following the 2008 recession.[54] Also, U.S. corporate profits have increased at an average annual rate of 7.9% per year during the last five years and 5.7% per year during the last ten years.[55] This gives credence to critics of the Federal Reserve Bank (the Fed) who say that the Fed's low-interest-rate policy has helped the ownership class thrive in recent years, while the middle class largely continues to struggle—that Main Street has not benefitted from the gains on Wall Street. This environment has squeezed the middle class. And, according to the Pew Research Center, in a report issued in December of 2015, after serving as the nation's majority for four decades, the middle class is now matched in size by the economic tiers above it and below it.

Not unexpectedly, people are adapting to the changing environment, but that creates its own dislocations. For example, older workers are staying in the workforce longer because they cannot afford to retire, but this can have the effect of dampening wages for younger, less-experienced workers who are eager to build their skill set. It's no wonder many people say things are tougher these days for both the middle class planning for retirement and those just starting out in their careers. A result of this tough job market is that it becomes more difficult to find money to set aside for retirement savings. And this is especially troublesome in an era where pensions are disappearing and workers have to fund their own retirements.

---

[54] *S&P 500 Index.* (n.d.). Morning Star. Retrieved from http://quicktake.morningstar.com/index/IndexCharts.aspx?Symbol=SPX (accessed 7 December 2015).

[55] *Corporate profits after tax (without IVA and CCAdj).* (n.d.). Economic Research: Federal Reserve Bank of St. Louis. Retrieved from https://research.stlouisfed.org/fred2/series/CP (accessed 7 December 2015).

The U.S. Census Bureau's main measure of inflation-adjusted median household income peaked in 1999 and 2000, fell in the 2001 recession, and never quite made it back to the old peak before falling again. The 2001 recession and the subsequent late 2007–2008 economic meltdown pretty much dashed many people's hopes for an increase in real wages. While the wealthy have apparently recovered from the recession and the economic fall, an August 2014 *Wall Street Journal* poll found that almost half of the people it surveyed feel the country is still in a recession, and more than 64% said they are still feeling the impact of the December 2007–June 2009 recession.[56] What might be surprising is this poll was taken more than five years after the last recession ended!

Unfortunately, there is a possibility that stagnant wages and a strong economic middle-class pinch may be here for a long time, despite what just about every politician may be promising. Therefore, given the sluggish wage growth, many people are beginning to supplement full-time wages with side businesses and second jobs in order to fund their financial goals and objectives.[57]

This has helped fuel the rise of what is being called the "gig economy," where individuals work in various part-time jobs, such as driving for Uber or Lyft. Other individuals and families reduce their lifestyle expenses, or begin to live beneath their means. Many get creative with ways to stretch their income while saving for their future. It is these extra steps and a commitment to realizing financial

---

[56] O'Connor, Patrick. (5 August 2014). *Poll finds widespread economic anxiety*. The Wall Street Journal. Retrieved from http://www.wsj.com/articles/wsj-nbc-poll-finds-widespread-economic-anxiety-1407277801

[57] Klimasinska, Kasia. (17 February 2014). *More workers take second jobs to bridge income gap*. Bloomberg News. Retrieved from https://www.bostonglobe.com/business/2014/02/17/more-workers-take-second-jobs-bridge-income-gap/T5QYGOYsJzRiYRADkHfpGP/story.html

freedom that may make a difference for many in what can otherwise be a very difficult journey to financial independence.

Alternatively, in such a difficult environment, there are some who ultimately will rely on the government safety net as part of their long-term plan. This can be a legitimate plan for millions of people. If you are looking into your financial future, and you are not optimistic about what you see and how you can change it, then, fortunately, you live in a country where there is a social safety net with food stamps, welfare, and government-paid health care and end-of-life care, as well as other benefits along the way. To the extent you earned credits during your work life, there will also be social security income at retirement age. If this is enough of a lifestyle for you, and the thought of or ability to save more is too intimidating, then solely relying on the government can be your strategy. For the tens of millions of Americans who have been unable to save, this has become their de facto strategy—whether it was planned or not. But before embarking on this strategy, please think very carefully about whether this is really what you want. Take note that you will have to be somewhat impoverished to benefit from the largess of the government, as these programs are designed for the neediest of families. There is little to no middle-class welfare.

Hurdle #2: Rising Costs of Health Care

In recent years, the cost of health care, whether it is through higher insurance premiums, higher co-pays, or higher deductibles, has continued to rise. These higher health-care costs are squeezing the cash flow of tens of millions of Americans, making less money available for their other goals.[58]

As a nation, we were hopeful that the much-ballyhooed healthcare reform would lower the cost of health care for the middle class, but that did not happen. To be fair, if the real goal of the health care bill (whether it was clearly stated or not) was to broaden coverage and offer more people the benefits of health insurance, then it appears to have been effective. If it was to lower health care costs for the middle class, then it is falling short of that goal. To think we were going to offer more people free or subsidized health insurance and that someone else wasn't going to pay for it was foolhardy, and the middle class is now feeling the pinch.

Of course someone has to pay for those who cannot afford to pay for their own insurance, and these costs have now shifted to just about everyone else in the system through higher premiums, co-pays, and deductibles. There were also some tax increases in the Affordable Care Act, which were designed to impact the "wealthy." But, generally, in our tax system, we tax income, not accumulated wealth. Therefore, many young professionals such as doctors and lawyers with massive student debt and a negative net worth may have been lumped into the "wealthy" category simply because they have high incomes. As a result, they are not only dealing with the higher insurance premiums and deductibles, they are also paying higher taxes that were designed for those with a higher net worth. Sure, if they are subject to these new taxes, they are earning a high income, but they may also be carrying significant debt. Their reward for

---

[58] Erickson, Jennifer. (24 September 2014). *The middle-class squeeze: A picture of stagnant incomes, rising costs, and what we can do to strengthen America's middle class.* Center for American Progress. Retrieved from https://www.americanprogress.org/issues/economy/report/2014/09/24/96903/the-middle-class-squeeze/

enduring years of additional education now includes being met with some of our country's highest tax rates—all this while sometimes having a negative net worth. That hardly seems fair, but such is the case when we say we are "taxing the wealthy."

While some might want to argue that health insurance premiums are declining, I don't meet many people who tell me they are paying less for insurance. The data also indicates rising insurance costs.[59] And worse yet, while many people are not only continuing to pay more for health insurance, they are also paying more for doctor visits due to higher out-of-pocket expenses, higher co-pays, and higher deductibles.[60] These deductibles are a real cost to a typical American family. The added cost for deductibles comes right out of what would otherwise be discretionary income that could be saved for retirement or financial freedom. Remember, when you add to your annual expenses, and your income remains stagnant, there is even less to save. Against this backdrop, we can see some of the reasons for the very low rate of saving among Americans.

Here is data illustrating what higher health-care costs look like: In 2014, the average insurance premium for a family of four, including both employer and employee contributions, was $16,834, or 31% of the median family income, up from 15% in 2003. The average deductibles also rose—from $518 in 2003 to almost $1,025 in 2010 and then to

---

[59] *Health insurance: premiums and increases.* (July 2015). National Conference of State Legislators. Retrieved from http://www.ncsl.org/research/health/health-insurance-premiums.aspx

[60] Ungar, Laura, & Jayne O'donnell. (1 January 2016). *Dilemma over deductibles: costs crippling middle-class.* USA Today. Retrieved from http://www.usatoday.com/story/news/nation/2015/01/01/middle-class-workers-struggle-to-pay-for-care-despite-insurance/19841235/

$1,217 in 2014. As a result, deductibles went from comprising 2% of a family's median income in 2003 to 3% by 2014.[61]

Hurdle #3: An Increasing Tax Burden

It's reasonable to assume that most Americans will be paying more taxes in the future (assuming they maintain at least a steady level of income). While there is little you can do about how your earned income is taxed, there are strategies you can use to reduce taxes on savings and investments. Therefore, your current savings and investment plans should be structured to address the potentially high tax burden. Taxes are harsh enough during your working years. However, the income and investment taxes during your retirement years are an often-overlooked aspect of the onerous tax structure many Americans face. In retirement, taxes on investments, social security, and your pension—if you are fortunate to have one—can set back the plans of many retirees.

It's all too easy to get political when it comes to taxes. Facts, however, can't be denied, regardless of politics. There are not enough mega-wealthy people to pay off the national debt and to fund the deficits.[62] Eventually, the higher tax burden falls on the middle class.

Why might tax rates rise? There are many reasons including the soaring U.S. budget deficit and rapidly growing entitlement costs of an aging population. Sooner or later, the bills have to be paid, and

---

[61] O'Donnell, Jayne. *Employer health plan deductibles see big 5-year jump.* (10 September 2014). USA Today. Retrieved from http://www.usatoday.com/story/news/nation/2014/09/10/employer-health-plans-deductibles-five-year-increase/15326741/ (accessed 22 June 2016).

[62] Frank, Robert. (15 August 2011). *Would taxing the super-rich raise much revenue?* Wall Street Journal. Retrieved from http://blogs.wsj.com/wealth/2011/08/15/would-taxing-the-super-rich-raise-much-revenue/

higher tax rates will most likely be part of the solution.[63] Taxes are necessary, of course. They pay for new schools and infrastructure, provide well-intentioned social programs for those in need, pay for defense, and fund basic necessities that we take for granted every day. We all benefit from government expenditures. But this doesn't change the reality that federal, state, and even local governments are spending more money than they are taking in, and what is more worrisome is that our government continues to make more promises or is unable to curtail the underfunded promises of the past. As a result, debt, as well as future obligations known as contingent liabilities, continues to be added. These contingent liabilities are not reflected in a current balance sheet, but are indeed future obligations that will cost taxpayers money.

Another reason taxes may continue to rise is the pending decline in the standard of living of millions of Americans. With tens of millions of baby boomers financially unprepared to stop working and pay for basic expenditures in retirement, the government might actually need to expand its social programs—not reduce them as some in Washington would prefer to see. In fact, with 60 million Americans reporting that they have no retirement savings, it might be that the government cannot reduce the amount and size of its social programs.[64]

Be wary if you hear politicians say that only the wealthy will pay more going forward. It is likely that the middle class may not be

---

[63] Kadlec, Dan. (24 August 2014). *Why higher future tax rates are certain, but won't matter.* Time. Retrieved from http://business.time.com/2012/08/24/why-higher-future-tax-rates-are-certain-but-wont-matter/

[64] Holland, Kelley. (13 April 2015). *Retiring well? Not most baby boomers.* CNBC. Retrieved from http://www.cnbc.com/2015/04/13/retiring-well-not-most-baby-boomers.html

exempt from future tax hikes and may well be asked to pay for some of the promises the government has made. Consider, for instance, the plight that middle-class Marylanders faced when their legislature passed the "Millionaires Tax." It would be logical to think that the Millionaire's Tax only kicked in at income levels of $1 million or more, but think again.[65] It kicked in at only $100,000 per year.[66]

Raising income tax is not the only means by which states and the federal government increase revenue. For instance, elimination and phase-out of tax deductions was a tactic used in the bipartisan American Taxpayer Relief Act of 2012 (passed by Congress and signed into law by President Obama in January 2013). Take also the Patient Protection and Affordable Care Act. It was chock full of revenue raises, such as new taxes on investments and higher Medicare taxes (and perhaps most crushingly, it brought on the higher deductibles that millions of Americans now pay for their health care and health insurance).[67]

As the federal government makes more promises and faces soaring budget deficits, prudent financial planning might include the expectation of higher federal income taxes. In addition, many state and local governments have also made expensive pension and benefit promises. States, unlike the federal government, have the obligation to balance their budgets. As a result, they will face the tough trade off of either reducing benefits or raising taxes.

---

[65] Frank, Robert. (9 July 2012). *In Maryland, higher taxes chase out rich: Study.* CNBC. Retrieved from http://www.cnbc.com/id/48120446

[66] Lazrick, Len. (11 June 2012). *Maryland imposes millionaire's tax on $100,000 incomes.* Heartland. Retrieved from http://news.heartland.org/newspaper-article/2012/06/11/maryland-imposes-millionaires-tax-100000-incomes

[67] Mayer, Kathryn. (26 November 2014). *High PPACA deductibles climbing higher.* BenefitsPro. Retrieved from http://www.benefitspro.com/2014/11/26/high-ppaca-deductibles-climbing-higher

In addition to higher income and property taxes, states like California and Maryland are harbingers of what else might be down the road in terms of creative ways that municipalities and states might add to their coffers. Even though these states already have some of the highest income tax rates in the nation, in the past few years they have both found creative measures to raise income from taxpayers. Maryland not only recently raised its gas tax, but also included an automatic inflation adjustment to the tax rate. Montgomery County, Maryland, has had success with their tax on grocery bags, and now other localities are looking to do the same. There is no shortage of unique taxes. For example, Illinois taxes candy that doesn't contain flour, New York taxes sliced bagels prepared *inside* a store, and Arkansas taxes tattoos.[68] If you take a look at your cable, power, or cell phone bills, you might be surprised how taxes sneak in there too. If you travel, your airfare, rental car, and hotel are loaded with extra costs. State and local taxes like these and others may be small, but they are levied on your after-tax income, and they add up. More importantly, they take away from money a middle class saver might otherwise invest in a savings or investment account. No wonder taxes are such a headwind against the financial plans of millions of hard-working Americans. And there is little sign of higher taxes abating.

Consider, for example, Illinois, which has a history of offering robust public-sector employee pension plans. Their Supreme Court recently ruled that the state is contractually bound to honor the $105 billion in pensions it has promised, regardless of the burden this

---

[68] *Top ten strangest state taxes*. (4 April 2012). Go Banking Rates, US News & World Report. Retrieved from http://money.usnews.com/money/blogs/my-money/2012/04/04/top-10-strangest-state-taxes

poses on the tax-paying public.[69] To be sure, the hard workers who earned those pensions and the automatic cost of living adjustments they were promised deserve to be paid—I am not disputing that. But this sort of economic tug-of-war is a story that will be played out more in the future as our leaders fail to lead, and the cost of promises made yesterday will be paid by the taxpayers of tomorrow. For the coming decades, younger workers will be face to face with the promises made by politicians in the past (some of whom may have been thinking about their short-term reelection plans and not looking at things like the cost of pensions in a world with longer life expectancies). Of course, state and local governments need to honor their promises, but as they continue to add the costs of future pension and benefit promises onto the backs of workers who do not have access to their own pensions, I believe private sector workers will increasingly take more notice.

> Wealth is often gained by spending less than you earn and then saving and growing the remainder.

As a financial planner, I see the tremendous impact of taxes on those who are trying to accumulate wealth. Other than gifts or an inheritance, wealth is often gained by spending less than you earn and then saving and growing the remainder. But before you have money to spend or save, you have to pay taxes. It is really a simple relationship: the higher the tax on your earned income, the less you have available to spend and save. After paying income taxes, your spending budget is further burdened by other taxes (e.g., property,

---

[69] Pearson, Rick, & Kim Geiger. (8 May 2015). *Illinois Supreme Court rules landmark pension law unconstitutional.* Chicago Tribune. Retrieved from http://www.chicagotribune.com/news/local/politics/ct-illinois-pension-law-court-ruling-20150508-story.html#page=1]

gasoline, and sales taxes). Obviously, the more we pay in taxes, the less we keep for ourselves and for our retirement savings plans.

In the event you are able to save, you are still not done with the taxman. The government will then tax the growth of your investments. By doing so, they are slowing down your wealth accumulation. It is akin to wearing ankle weights and trying to run. Think about a typical person running versus a person running with a 10-pound weight on each ankle. All else being equal, the person with the extra burden will lag. This is why taxes on your investments are a real drag.

Later in life, such as in retirement when an investor is no longer focusing on accumulation of wealth (the accumulation phase), but rather spending their wealth (the distribution phase), the tax burden doesn't stop. During this distribution phase, withdrawals from 401(k) plans, CD and bond interest, and pension income are all subject to ordinary income tax. And even a majority of your social security can be taxed at your ordinary income tax rates. For most retirees, it's hard to avoid ordinary income tax rates, which are typically the highest cost structure of the personal income tax code. Some exceptions are long-term capital gains (those investments that increased and were held for more than 12 months)[70] and certain qualified dividends that qualify for a lower tax rate. However, even these somewhat favorable rates are being questioned as favoring the wealthy and are being considered for a phase out or for an increase. Depending on the income level at which these higher taxes would start, they could have an impact on the growth of the assets a middle-class investor has managed to accumulate.

---

[70] *Definition of long-term, capital gain.* (n.d.). Investopedia. Retrieved from http://www.investopedia.com/terms/l/long-term_capital_gain_loss.asp (Accessed 22 June 2016).

In January 2013, the capital gains rate did, in fact, increase from 15% to 20% for many higher earners. In addition, the Patient Protection and Affordable Care Act also added a 3.8% tax to most investment income, such as capital gains and interest income, provided your adjusted gross income was more than $200,000 a year as a single person or $250,000 as a couple. These income levels may be beyond what is considered middle class, but these income-tax thresholds could be lowered in the future. If historical tendencies are our guide, and if the promises of the Affordable Care Act become more costly, this might be the case. Looking forward, there is a growing movement of activists and politicians who are proposing sharp increases in the tax on capital gains and on short-term investments. While this action may also have the benefit of shifting the current, short-term focus of some American investors to more long-term interests, it would nevertheless be another tax on your investment gains.[71]

One possible tax change to keep an eye out for: the potential phase-out or reduction of the $250,000 capital-gains exemption on the sale of a personal residence. This exemption doubles to $500,000 for a married couple and is, of course, subject to a wide range of rules and circumstances. In this situation, a couple could conceivably exclude a $500,000 capital gain on the sale of their personal residence. As we increasingly hear of a world where we want more tax fairness and less loopholes (for the wealthy), I am not optimistic that this "loophole" will last indefinitely. If you find yourself saying something like, "I have a nice gain in my home's value, but I don't consider myself wealthy," you would not be alone. But the reality is that, to the cash-strapped U.S. Treasury, having a $250,000 gain might mean you are indeed

---

[71] Meckler, Laura. (24 July 2015). *Hillary Clinton proposes sharp rise in some capital-gains tax rates.* The Wall Street Journal. Retrieved from http://www.wsj.com/articles/clinton-to-propose-rise-in-capital-gains-taxes-on-short-term-investments-1437747732

"rich." Many people nearing retirement who downsized and sold their longtime residence have used this benefit. If the exemption is removed, all your realized gains on your home may be subject to taxes.

As with any tax situation, you should consult your tax advisor. Each situation is unique, and the tax code is complex. Please look at your situation with your tax advisor before deciding to sell your home in advance of any possible phase out of the valuable exemption.

Hurdle #4: A Rising Cost of Living

Inflation, which is almost always present in our economy, simply means that your money will continue to buy less as time passes. Once you understand how inflation impacts your purchasing power, you may choose to adjust your savings and revenue plans upward.

Inflation is a slippery thing to define exactly. I've defined it here as the increase in prices and a corresponding fall in the purchasing value of money. An easy way to think of inflation is to consider what $20 can buy you now versus what it could have bought you twenty years ago. As inflation goes up, the cost of living goes up, because the main thing that inflation affects is the price of goods—not necessarily wages. So, for example, a 3% inflation-rate increase may not result in an automatic 3% increase in your wages. And even if you are fortunate enough to get an inflation-based wage increase, that raise doesn't mean you're making more money in real terms. It just means that you're now able to keep up with inflation.

The trouble with inflation is that, because you don't notice it while it's happening, it can be hard to believe that it's real or that it is happening at all. Unlike the hyperinflation in the Weimar Republic (Germany) prior to World War II, where people resorted to carting around wheelbarrows of money, inflation usually is not dramatic. It normally happens slowly over time, so people often don't think it's a big deal. But inflation *is* a big deal. It is insidious in the way it creeps up. It's like gaining weight. You don't notice how much you're gaining from day to day. You think the dryer shrunk your pants or they're tight from the big meal you just ate. But one day you look in the mirror and think, *holy mackerel, what happened?* Well, it's the same with inflation. We don't notice that the price of milk has gone up a few cents every month, but the reality is that milk cost about $2.26 per gallon in 1984, and in 2015, it was around $3.86. If you hadn't bought milk for 30 years and you decide to pick up a gallon for the family, you might be in for a surprise.

If you compare what some items cost today (e.g., milk, postage stamps, coffee, automobiles, and housing) with what they cost in past decades, you'll notice a distinct difference. For example, in the last 27 years, with an average inflation rate of nearly 2.66% overall, prices have more than doubled.[72] If prices continue to rise at the same rate, we can expect prices to double *again* in the next 27 years. Here I will describe how to calculate the number of years it takes for prices to double at a given inflation rate. It is a handy tool known as the "Rule of 72." This Rule of 72 can also help you estimate the number of years it will take for your investments to double.

The Rule of 72

In order to find the number of years required to double the cost of living or double your money at a given inflation or interest rate, divide 72 by the inflation or investment return rate. The result is the approximate number of years that it will take for prices to double (using an inflation rate) or your investment to double (using an

---

[72] *Consumer Price Index 1913*. (n.d.). Federal Reserve Bank of Minneapolis. Retrieved from https://www.minneapolisfed.org/community/teaching-aids/cpi-calculator-information/consumer-price-index-and-inflation-rates-1913 (accessed 22 June 2016).

investment rate of return). This is what is known as the "Rule of 72." For example, using the Rule of 72, and assuming a 2.66% inflation rate, today's 40-year-old will see the cost of living double in 27 years (72 ÷ 2.66 = 27). So, prices will double for this 40-year-old by the time he or she is on the cusp of full social security retirement age. Likewise, using the Rule of 72 and estimating that inflation is going to be 2.4%, then the cost of living will double in 30 years (72 ÷ 2.4 = 30), and this 40-year-old will be looking at a doubling of the cost of living by the time he or she is 70. The lower the inflation rate, the more beneficial it will be for retirees, as their expected costs might drop and annual income need may drop.

According to the Bureau of Labor Statistics (BLS), in 2014, the inflation rate was only 1.6%, which is very low by historical standards. It declined even further in 2015, but that was fueled by a sharp decline in oil prices, much of which was quickly reversed. Generally speaking, investors and retirees prefer lower inflation rates. However, there is a flip side to extremely low inflation: very low inflation usually coincides with low economic growth. Low economic growth leads the Fed, in an effort to stimulate economic growth, to keep interest rates low. These low interest rates punish savers (and retirees) who have money in savings accounts. For example, for the past several years and into 2016, the vast majority of bank money market accounts are hovering around 1% or even lower.[73] So even though inflation was relatively low at 1.6%, bank money market accounts at less than 1% offered savers a negative real rate of return and the low rate of interest they earned was also taxed!

The valuable planning point here is this: if the rate of return on your savings is below the rate of inflation, then you are earning what

---

[73] Latham, Saundra. (12 May 2016). *Best money market account for 2016*. The Simple Dollar. Retrieved from http://www.thesimpledollar.com/best-money-market-account/

we call a "negative real rate of return," and you are losing purchasing power! This is one reason why the Fed's current low-interest-rate policy is hurting so many savers and retirees. While in the long run, low inflation can be a positive for those accumulating assets and saving for retirement, low inflation can also lead to very low yields on savings accounts. This can work against someone at or near retirement age, as this group tends to look for lower-risk savings accounts as a part of their overall investment mix. Interestingly, Millennials and the younger Gen Xers also tend to be risk averse.[74] These two groups were first introduced to stocks during the tech crash of 2000, and then they lived through the subsequent "lost decade." During the ten-year period between January 2000 and December 2009, the S&P 500 had a net loss of 9.1%.[75]

> If the rate of return on your savings is below the rate of inflation, then you are earning what we call a "negative real rate of return," and you are losing purchasing power!

The interest of younger people in stock market investing has been surprisingly tepid. Unfortunately for them, if they are staying in cash, the yields are not keeping up with inflation. Between 1999 and 2014, inflation averaged 2.23%. At this relatively low inflation rate, the cost of living can potentially double in just over 32 years.[76] Now, this may seem like a long time and not much of a concern. But let's say you're

---

[74] Russolillo, Steven. (29 May 2014). *Chart of the day: Millennials are really risk averse.* The Wall Street Journal. Retrieved from http://blogs.wsj.com/moneybeat/2014/05/29/chart-of-the-day-millennials-are-really-risk-averse/

[75] *Definition of lost decade.* (n.d.). Investopedia. Retrieved from http://www.investopedia.com/terms/l/lost-decade.asp (accessed 22 June 2016).

[76] *Current U.S. inflation rates 2005–2015.* (n.d.). U.S. Inflation Calculator, CoinNews Media. Retrieved from http://www.usinflationcalculator.com/inflation/current-inflation-rates/ (accessed 7 December 2015).

33 years old, and you're saving for retirement, and you think you want to live on $100,000 a year, plus whatever social security will provide. Adjusted for inflation, when you're 65, you may need to generate $200,000 per year to maintain a similar standard of living to what you enjoy today. And, using our 4% sustainable withdrawal rate (as defined in chapter 1), you will need to have accumulated $5,000,000 to generate $200,000 of income at age 65. This underscores the magnitude of the challenge for young people, and why starting to save early is so important. Furthermore, if inflation rises above this 2.23% rate, then $200,000 may not be enough income, which is why I consider inflation to be one of the biggest obstacles a young investor faces.

Like our hypothetical 33-year-old saver in this example, if you want the same standard of living that you have now when you're age 65, you must factor in the impact of inflation. To be sure, your lifestyle might simplify, and your actual spending needs may be less than they are currently, but your living expenses might also rise, particularly if you're in an assisted living community, have health care issues, or if you have out-of-state grandchildren you want to see a lot of, and so on. For these and other reasons, I do not suggest people set a goal of having a significantly lower future cost of living. And, what kind of goal would it be to aim low? Instead, I suggest including an inflation assumption and keeping a reasonable expectation of your current lifestyle in retirement.

People often underestimate the impact of inflation when considering how many assets they need to accumulate for retirement. My guess is most people didn't work hard their whole life to take a 50% pay cut. Yet, that's what a 43-year-old couple who are currently spending $120,000 a year would be doing when they try to live on that same $120,000 at age 67 if inflation averaged 3%. To keep up with this hypothetical 3% inflation rate, this couple will need to generate $240,000 in 24 years. If we don't count social security, in order to generate this $240,000 (and if we use our 4% sustainable withdrawal rate), this couple would need to have about $6 million dollars saved in order to maintain their lifestyle. Of course, including social security income means this $6 million figure can be lower. Using a hypothetical $40,000 in annual social security payments, these retirees would need to generate $200,000 from investments. In this case, using our sustainable withdrawal rate of 4%, roughly $5 million in assets would be needed to generate $200,000 of target income. Still a very sizable portfolio!

Dealing with inflation is part of the middle-class challenge. And while inflation has been, by historical standards, relatively low coming out of the recent great recession, it remains one of the greatest enemies of investors and retirees.[77] One way to combat the impacts of inflation is to start saving when you are young so you can benefit from compounding growth on your savings. The Rule of 72 can also help you estimate the future value of your investments. If, for example, you assume that you can earn a very ambitious 10% compound rate of return on your money, it will double in 7.2 years (72 / 10 = 7.2). If you earn 8% on your money, it will double in 9 years (72 / 8 = 9), and if you earn 6% on your money, it will double in 12 years (72 / 6 = 12).

This rule is factoring in "compound interest." Compound interest is interest calculated on the initial principal and also on the

---

[77] Kiley, Michael T. (23 November 2015). *Low inflation in the United States: A summary of recent research*. FEDS Notes, Federal Reserve. Retrieved from http://www.federalreserve.gov/econresdata/notes/feds-notes/2015/low-inflation-in-the-united-states-a-summary-of-recent-research-20151123.html

accumulated interest of previous periods. Compound interest can be thought of as "interest on interest."

It is reasonable to assume that one of the goals of most investors is to target a rate of return in excess of the rate of inflation. This is not as easy as it sounds because investing brings out a range of emotions from most investors. People have a desire not to lose their money, yet they need to earn more than the rate of inflation or they risk losing purchasing power. This is a challenge especially for lower-risk investors, like near retirees, who still may have long life expectancies and who need to grow their portfolios ahead of inflation or risk running out of money prematurely. They are faced with the decision to invest in potential growth investments that also carry higher risks in an effort to earn more than the inflation rate. This challenge is being made even more difficult during a period of relatively low interest rates on savings accounts, money markets, and CDs.

Low Interest Rates Are Creating Distortions

Consider that the average 5-year CD interest rate was 6.0% in 2000.[78] In comparison, the average 5-year CD rate pays much lower at just 0.8% in 2016.[79] How are these current low rates affecting retirees? Those who are earning just enough money to get by may be afraid to risk losing any money, so they stay in an FDIC-insured bank account, such as a CD, and earn far less than in the past. Or they go upstream in the risk market to chase a higher yield in an attempt to fund their lifestyle.

---

[78] *CD rates history.* (n.d.). Bankrate. Retrieved from http://www.bankrate.com/finance/cd-rates-history-0112.aspx (accessed 22 June 2015).

[79] *CD rates: 5-year certification of deposit.* (n.d.). Economic Research, Federal Reserve Bank of St. Louis. Retrieved from https://research.stlouisfed.org/fred2/series/CD60NRJD (accessed 12 May 2016).

These current, historically-low rates are creating some distortions, and we haven't yet seen the full potential fallout. For example, let's say your Aunt Sally had $1 million in her bank account about 15 years ago. At a 6% interest rate, she earned approximately $60,000 per year in CD interest and paid her expenses. But as her CD's interest rate declined, eventually it would not have kept up with inflation. In fact, it would have dropped to less than 1%, causing a decline in her income and purchasing power. If she stayed in the CD with her $1,000,000, her CD interest would have plunged from $60,000 per year to less than $10,000 per year. Given this decline, what can Aunt Sally do to keep her income up? In all likelihood, if she wanted to live on the same nominal amount of income she used to generate from her bank accounts, she might have considered chasing higher-risk investments. After all, higher returns usually mean higher risk. This shift, where individuals are almost forced to go to higher-risk investments to maintain cash flow, is an unintended consequence of the low-interest-rate policy of the Fed. What is concerning is that we have not seen all the damage that still might play out.

If Aunt Sally is now invested in higher-risk assets to chase higher yield, she may not have yet felt the pain of a future stock market correction or a deteriorating bond market. But if and when interest rates rise, or when asset values decline, and Aunt Sally is no longer invested in an FDIC-insured product, those higher-risk investments will likely be impacted—to what degree is as yet unknown. Aunt Sally has the following three basic choices:

1. Keep her money in her bank account, earning about 1%, and live on far less than she has been.
2. Chase higher-yield (with higher-risk) investments in an attempt to maintain her lifestyle.

3. Cannibalize principal and spend down her hard-earned assets, increasing the risk of running out of money sooner than she hoped.

She might choose any one or a combination of the three choices, but the low-interest-rate environment is forcing some difficult decisions.

Summary

Maintaining your way of life and your ability to save for retirement is adversely affected by many factors, including stagnant wages and underemployment, higher health care costs, rising taxes, and an increased cost of living. These factors may make it difficult to have the sort of middle-class or affluent lifestyle enjoyed by previous generations. Investors have the challenge of first finding the extra discretionary income to save, then deciding on where to invest it in a low-interest-rate environment while targeting a rate of return greater than the rate of inflation. Also, taxes will need to be managed on any investment gain or income. In order to give yourself the best chance against these challenges, you must knowledgeably plan for the life and financial freedom/retirement you want, and then implement the discipline and strategies you will need to counter these negative forces.[80] Here are some steps to consider:

---

[80] FDIC insurance does not cover other financial products and services that banks may offer, such as stocks, bonds, mutual funds, life insurance policies, annuities, or securities. The standard insurance amount is $250,000 per depositor, per insured bank, for each account ownership category.

- Make a commitment early in your adult life to gain the financial success you want to enjoy.

- Build your skill set to succeed in a challenging and changing economy.

- To overcome stagnant wages, consider adding additional income streams in the form of a second job or a side business.

- If possible, seek out opportunities with companies that offer generous stock grant programs and other ownership opportunities.

- Carefully consider which type of health care coverage is best for you and your family. Combining a higher deductible plan with a Health Savings Account (HSA) may work well if you don't expect to need a lot of medical care. Heavier users of medical care might want to look at lower deductibles even though premiums might be higher. This is a complex area, and each situation is unique, so consult with a professional.

- Increase your knowledge of how you pay for health care, and take proactive steps to reduce its cost. For example, in this new environment of high deductibles, try to plan your optional medical care outlays more efficiently. If it's late in the year, and you still have a large deductible remaining, consider scheduling routine exams and non-urgent procedures early the following year.

- Become a more active partner with your tax professional in devising ways to ensure your tax profile and obligations are as lean as you can comfortably make them. Also work with your investment professional, or learn more about how you can reduce the income taxes on your investments.

) Educate yourself on how taxes impact wealth accumulation. Then develop strategies for your unique situation.

) Examine your current expense picture realistically, and look for ways to reduce unnecessary expenses.

) If you are married or partnered in a family or household unit, strategize how each individual's existing and potential financial contributions will factor into your current savings mix and your retirement planning. Teamwork can make a big difference to a couple's financial success.

) Estimate the impact of inflation and how your savings goal might be bigger than you think. Inflation adds an additional hurdle in your journey toward financial freedom, so you need to take it head on, and save and invest accordingly.

) Understand what a real rate of return is and focus on an effective long-term investment strategy. The axiom, "The greater the risk, the greater the potential return," is usually true for very long periods of time, like retirement planning. To the extent your personal risk tolerance allows for it, invest with that in mind.

CHAPTER 5

Avoiding the Middle-Class Traps (EASY)

Research shows that financial comfort does not necessarily lead to personal happiness.[81] It's also been shown that economic achievement, class status, or financial success do not equate to, guarantee, or assure happiness.[82] The reality is that wealth accumulation, like career choice, is not a universal goal or one-size-fits-all achievement. Financial status is only one aspect of each person's individual criteria for happiness. Everyone has his or her own unique needs, dreams, and desires. Effective financial planning is about helping people with their own specific goals and dreams.

There are many reasons why some people become more financially successful than others. To a large extent however, earned income is

---

[81] Popick, Susie. (9 June 2014). *The money-happiness connection: Does money buy happiness?* Money. Retrieved from http://time.com/money/2802147/does-money-buy-happiness/

[82] *Respect matters more than money for happiness in life.* (20 June 2012). Association for Psychological Science. Retrieved from http://www.psychologicalscience.org/index.php/news/releases/respect-from-friends-matters-more-than-money-for-happiness-in-life.html

a key way that some can transcend their family-of-origin's economic status. A good college degree and hard work still suffice for many people, and good fortune occasionally shines on some who get the right job at the right time and see their careers take off. For example, think about the junior finance person or executive assistant who answered an ad in *The Washington Post* for a position at a small startup in Northern Virginia called America Online (AOL), or a mid-level executive who worked for Microsoft during the 1980s. I remember walking through AOL's offices and meeting administrative assistants who had close to a million dollars in AOL stock (I just hope they sold it at a good time). Still others do it the old-fashioned way: either marrying into wealth or inheriting it. There is not just one way to become wealthy. But one thing is certain, and that is avoiding bad money-management habits will help just about everyone.

Over the years, I have noticed a consistent pattern of financial traps that people fall into. There are many, but I am listing here four of the big ones that I see frequently. To help you understand and avoid these four traps, I have placed them into easy-to-remember acronym, EASY:

1. Entitlement
2. Aspirational Purchases
3. Short-Term Thinking
4. Yes to Almost Everything

Some of us will be susceptible to some or even all of these; while others will easily be able to avoid them once they're pointed out. We each have different psychological needs and think differently about money. A trap that seems obvious to you, might not be so obvious to someone else, and vice versa.

In her poem about a hole in the sidewalk, singer-songwriter-actress-author Portia Nelson gives us a great analogy about avoiding traps. The basic idea is this:

> One day you're walking down a street and fall into a hole. Frustrated, you climb out and go on your way. The next day you're walking down the same street, pretend you don't see the hole, fall in again, and have to climb out again! The third day you notice the hole but fall in, anyway, out of habit. The fourth day you finally walk around the hole. And on the fifth day, you really get wise and take a different route altogether!

That's how many of us are with money and spending. We tend to fall into certain behaviors over and over again. But armed with a written financial plan, it may become easier to recognize the traps, avoid the traps, and chart a better course.

If you recognize that one or more of the following traps apply to you, you have just taken the first step to avoiding them in the future. The number one principle in all of these traps is to *not* ignore them. Instead, face them head on. Gaining affluence and financial success often starts with living within your means. While it sounds easy, living within your means is often difficult for many people. Know that if you sometimes struggle to put aside the amount you need to save each month, you are not alone. Let's review these four traps to see how they might apply to your current situation.

E = Entitlement

Whether it's the latest gadget, a designer wardrobe, a new car, or a vacation home, many people who have worked hard to make good money feel they've earned the right to spend their money as they please. They *have* earned the right. The challenge is finding a balance between spending on what you think you are entitled to while not forgetting the financial goals you have set for yourself.

When you believe in this kind of entitlement without discipline, you might start thinking, "Gosh, I'm making $150,000 a year. This is way more money than I thought I would make when I was in college. And I have $400,000 in the bank. That's a lot of money. My boss has a Porsche, and my buddies go to Vegas every year. Now that I earn a lot, I want to do those things, too." Or, if you've come into an inheritance or unexpected windfall, you might say, "I deserve to spend that 'found money' since I wasn't planning on having it in the first place. Why save it for the future instead of enjoying it now?"

The truth is, you do have every right to spend your money. However, if you are behind on your financial goals and want financial freedom in the long run, then now may be a good time to save. That way, later in life when your earned income is reduced or stops altogether, you can still generate sufficient cash flow from your investments to live the life you want. Finding a balance consistent with an overall plan might allow for both present-day enjoyment and future wealth. One opportunity to do this is to save any unexpected bonuses or inheritances. Avoid the temptation to spend these simply because you can.

Depression-era families and those with parents who lived through the Depression usually understand the importance of saving. They know that spending freely isn't the wisest way to control money and can likely jeopardize their financial future. They also know that having extra cash helps to diminish financial stress. However, many people have a different reference point or didn't learn about the need to save from their parents or grandparents. Others may know about the benefit of saving, but choose to ignore it.

In 2013, the National Retirement Risk Index, which measures Americans' retirement preparedness, found that 52% of American households were at risk of being unable to maintain their present standard of living through their retirement.[83] And in a 2014 Harris poll, at least 74% of those surveyed cited worries about having enough income during retirement.[84] That's a lot of people out there who are worried about their financial health and future.

If you cannot limit your spending or find some cash to save, ask yourself, "Why?" Like a lot of people, you may have trouble balancing your long-term goals with your short-term wants. Satisfying your short-term wants may be a form of entitlement. Psychologists, the media, and heavy spenders often refer to unplanned and sometimes reckless spending as "retail therapy addiction." The effects of spending sprees are well known and well documented. Reckless spending typical of a shopping spree can bring an endorphin rush. Buying things we don't need but want (for whatever reason) excite the brain's neurochemicals. During shopping sprees, a special part of the brain floods the body with dopamine, the same chemical that's released during sex and

> Reckless spending typical of a shopping spree can bring an endorphin rush.

---

[83] *National retirement risk index.* (n.d.). Center for Retirement Research at Boston College. Retrieved from http://crr.bc.edu/special-projects/national-retirement-risk-index/ (accessed 12 June 2016).

[84] Holland, Kelley. (23 March 2015). *Retirement crisis: The great 401(k) experiment has failed for many Americans.* NBC News. Retrieved from http://www.nbcnews.com/business/retirement/great-401-k-experiment-has-failed-many-americans-n327321

cocaine use.[85] It's no wonder spending money makes us feel good. One in 20 Americans has a retail therapy addiction so serious it jeopardizes their relationships, jobs, and sometimes even their lives.[86] A recent study conducted by TNS Global found that more than 50% of Americans admit to engaging in retail therapy.[87] This kind of internal hormonal response also occurs after eating chocolate and after exercising. No wonder spending can be addictive![88] Pair that rush of hormones with entitlement thinking, and it can be easy to see why saving is so difficult for so many people.

A = Aspirational Purchases

Aspirational purchases are those you make because you believe they will help you gain recognition or status. However, if you are purchasing status items to the degree that your overall financial foundation is in jeopardy, then you are aspiring to a lifestyle that you cannot afford. It will catch up to you in the long run.

Numerous studies have sought to understand *why* people fall prey to aspirational purchasing. Psychotherapist Will Meyerhofer explains that a person may purchase a luxury item, such as a Porsche, not because he wants to take it on a racetrack but because he wants to be seen driving it. One comprehensive survey found that the conspicuous consumption of "high-status goods" acts to boosts one's

---

[85] Svoboda, Elizabeth. (1 September 2010) *Field Guide to the Shopaholic*. Psychology Today. Retrieved from https://www.psychologytoday.com/articles/201010/field-guide-the-shopaholic

[86] Ibid.

[87] Yarrow, Ph.D., Kit. (2 May 2013). *Why "retail therapy" works*. Psychology Today. Retrieved from https://www.psychologytoday.com/blog/the-why-behind-the-buy/201305/why-retail-therapy-works

[88] Ibid.

self-esteem and comes from a need both to signal wealth status and to protect weak self-esteem.[89] It's like needing to wear the same clothes and having the same hairstyle as the cool kids in high school.

Problems arise when this type of spending becomes systemic and persistent and negatively impacts our financial future. Aspirational spending reflects a detachment from living within one's means and undermines the most important aspect of planning for retirement: *saving*. Aspirational buyers represent the largest demographic of people purchasing nonessential goods and services. On average, 38% of shoppers in America are aspirational purchasers.[90] Seventy percent of them make aspirational purchases because spending and buying things just makes them feel better.[91]

The media and a pervasive culture of material consumerism commonly encourage this phenomenon. Advertisers love these aspirational buying guys and gals (they number equally by gender) because of their collective size and the potential they present for sustainable consumption.[92] They are a retailer's dream, and the marketing world makes it a mission to get them to spend more and feel good doing it.

---

[89] Sivanathan, Niro & Nathan C. Pettit. (4 February 2010) *Protecting the self through consumption: Status goods as affirmational commodities*. Journal of Experimental Social Psychology 46 (2010) 564–570. Retrieved from http://faculty.london.edu/nsivanathan/pdf/Sivanathan%20&%20Pettit%20(2010).pdf

[90] Generational Roadmap. (October 2012). *Re: thinking consumption: Consumers & the future of sustainability*. The Regeneration Roadmap. Retrieved from http://theregenerationroadmap.com/reports.html#/rethinking-consumption-consumer-study.html

[91] Godelnik, Raz. (3 December 2012). *7 things you need to know about aspirational consumers*. Triple Pundit. http://www.triplepundit.com/2012/12/aspirational-consumers/

[92] Ibid.

A written financial plan can help you better understand the benefits of deferring such purchases in exchange for real wealth later. Knowing how much you need to save each month in order to pursue your goals can be your strongest defense against the media's very compelling message to "Spend, spend, spend!" A written plan can also help couples get on "the same page," which further helps them jointly manage their spending. It also provides them with guidance and can preempt or mitigate arguments around money.

With a written financial plan, both partners understand that the purchase they are considering may not be a part of what they mutually agreed to. If you have a financial plan, and you know, for instance, that you need to save $3,000 a month, then when you're looking at that new $2,000 sound system, maybe you will be more cognizant of what that purchase means for your future. As the Doughertys said to each other, "What will we do with this new couch when we buy our sailboat?" They brought their plans for retirement into their present reality and opted to delay gratification so they could retire and live on a sailboat in the future. Living within their means helped them live the life they had imagined for themselves further down the road.

Once you begin to tap into that discipline consistently, then you will feel good knowing that you have an option in front of you other than spending. If your goal is to save for a well-funded retirement, then when you feel the urge to make an impulse buy, you can ask yourself: is this purchase really necessary? Sometimes the answer will be yes. If so, then enjoy the purchase—and maybe you can also think creatively about how to lower the price tag!

S = Short-Term Thinking

Short-term thinking is when people think only about the near term and spend without regard for the possibility of living a long life. In recent years, the concept of longevity risk—the risk that you will run out of money because you'll live longer than expected—is gaining traction among social economists. Without planning for a long life, you might find yourself experiencing longevity risk and being economically vulnerable when you have the least ability to earn a living and fend for yourself. No wonder one of the biggest fears among soon-to-retire Baby Boomers is running out of money; only 27% of them were confident they had enough money to last through their entire retirement.[93]

As a financial planner, I try to help people balance both the short-term desires for enjoyment with the necessity of planning for a long life. In discussions with clients about their cash flow, I make sure a portion of their after-tax income is designated for fun. A spending plan should never be equated with deprivation. A plan that doesn't allow for some enjoyment along the way will likely have a low probability of success. Much like deciding to eat a healthy diet to lose weight, an occasional splurge or some planned luxuries may actually help you stay on track.

An objective of a cash-flow worksheet inside an overall financial plan is to help structure household income in a way that allocates an amount for enjoying life while also saving for your financial future. A basic and effective cash-flow worksheet calculates your monthly after-tax income minus your monthly expenses. The remainder, also called discretionary income, is the amount of excess monthly cash flow that is available for saving. Saving a portion of your discretionary income is the cornerstone of a workable, sustainable, and effective plan that will help take you into the kind of retirement you aspire to

---

[93] Holland, Kelley. (13 April 2015). *Retiring well? Not most baby boomers.* CNBC. Retrieved from http://www.cnbc.com/2015/04/13/retiring-well-not-most-baby-boomers.html

achieve. By striking a spending-saving balance, you fund both the fun part of your spending plan *and* the savings component. For many, there eventually is significant joy and satisfaction in seeing savings balances increase.

Financial advisors should not tell you how to spend your income, but they may be able to help you adhere to the savings plan that you developed after completing your cash flow worksheet. Whenever possible, I use the term "cash-flow worksheet" and not "budget." I have noticed that I get a different response by asking clients about their monthly cash flow and spending plan than I get when I ask about a monthly budget. Budgets can feel restrictive, like a diet—and no one wants to be on a diet.

Unfortunately, many people are not able to accurately complete their own cash-flow worksheet. At the end of this book, in Appendix B, you'll find an easy-to-use sample of a cash-flow worksheet. Oftentimes, a person or couple tells me they spend far less than they actually do. For example, I routinely hear how little is spent each month relative to net, after-tax earnings. However, when I ask if this surplus can be automatically invested (instead of spent), I am met with resistance.

This is the point in the conversation when I realize that this person or couple doesn't know exactly where that money is being spent. The challenge now is to determine if the money is going toward necessary expenses or if it's being frittered away. If the latter, then there is unnecessary spending which is negatively impacting their financial goals and ultimately, their financial freedom. Often in these conversations, there is a "lightbulb moment" when my clients realize they're missing an opportunity to think beyond immediate gratification. They understand that they've fallen victim to the trap of short-term thinking.

Of course, not everyone I talk with has this "moment of truth" about their situation, but many do. And this one, simple realization can make a big difference. Some people say, "Wow, I didn't realize I had more money that I could save; let's start saving it each month." Setting aside this amount each month on an automatic basis can be a major step toward the success of your long-term financial plan. As the old saying goes, "Pay yourself first."

Y = Yes to Everything

When it comes to spending, do you find yourself saying "yes" more often than you know you should? Many people do, especially in the face of peer pressure, which is where a lot of excess spending can start.[94] When we see our friends and acquaintances spending money on things like private schools, an extra vacation, or a new car every few years, it's easy to desire similar things. For many people, however, those kinds of luxuries may be beyond their true financial capacity. And yet some of them are still saying "yes" to everything.

Saying "no" can be difficult, even under the best of circumstances. If you live in an upscale zip code, surrounded by affluence, you may find it even harder to resist the urge to live a bigger lifestyle. You hear the neighbors talk about their new kitchen, or awesome, new widescreen television, or over-the-top landscaping, and you may inwardly strive to keep up. What's worse, if you're already struggling with a sense of entitlement, aspirational purchases, or short-term thinking, you're going to have an even bigger challenge when affluence appears to be the norm, and you feel like you're falling behind.

---

[94] Furnham, Ph.D., Adrian. (5 December 2014). *Compulsive buying: What causes shopaholism? Why do some people seem consumed by spending?* Psychology Today. Retrieved from https://www.psychologytoday.com/blog/sideways-view/201412/compulsive-buying

One area where no one wants to "fall behind" is their child's or children's education. As a parent myself, I especially understand how we all want to say "yes" when it comes to providing the best for our kids. Considering whether to send your kids to private high school or private college is a deeply personal decision. I've known many parents who are behind on meeting their financial goals, yet still send their kids to private elementary and private high schools. It's certainly their right to do so, but measured against their other, underfunded goals, such as funding their own retirement, I am not sure how much sense this makes in the long run—especially in many affluent zip codes where a highly-rated, quality, public education appears to be available.

And then there's college. Paying for college also puts a serious strain on the finances of many middle-class and affluent families. While there are loan programs available, parents often wind up paying off the loans themselves. All too often, parents who are significantly underfunded toward their own goals are saying "yes" to spending tens of thousands or even a hundred thousand dollars or more on higher education for their kids. The impact to a parent's retirement plan is even worse when the parents are a little older and just a few years away from a significantly underfunded retirement

Of course, there are times a private college, or an expensive out-of-state public college education will be far more beneficial to a motivated, focused child who is working hard on a career-based major. But unfortunately, there are times where parents send their children to expensive colleges even when their children have no idea what their long-term plans are. And sometimes a change in their major turns their four-year plan into a five-year plan. Or sometimes they graduate with a major that they enjoyed studying, but it offers them very little in terms of job placement or a meaningful career.

This may be fine for a wealthy family who can set up a trust fund to support their free-spirited child for the next 70 years. But for a working family who may be behind on other financial goals and who may have other children heading off to college, it doesn't make a lot of sense. Keep in mind too, if you send your first child to a private school, it can be harder to tell your younger children they must attend a lower-cost state school.

Private college is very expensive. According to both the College Board and the National Center for Education Statistics, the average cost of attending full-time private college can total $45,000 per year at a private college. And those costs can soar to $50,000 or more at some colleges like Tulane,[95] Harvard,[96] or Caltech,[97] and even $60,000 at colleges like Stanford.[98] A family could be looking at costs of $85,000 to $100,000 or more per year if they have two children wanting to attend any of the top-tier private colleges.[99]

All this said, the middle-class deserves some sympathy regarding educational opportunities. Even when a family has a strong household income and lives modestly, oftentimes they have little left over to

---

[95] *Tuition & fees.* (n.d.). Undergraduate Admission, Tulane University. Retrieved from http://admission.tulane.edu/aid/tuition.php (accessed 30 April 2016).

[96] *Cost of attendance.* (n.d.). Harvard College Griffin Financial Aid Office, Harvard College. Retrieved from https://college.harvard.edu/financial-aid/how-aid-works/cost-attendance (accessed 30 April 2016).

[97] *Cost of attendance.* (n.d.) Caltech Admissions, Caltech. Retrieved from https://finaid.caltech.edu/costs (accessed 30 April 2016).

[98] *Tuition & fees: 2015–16 tuition schedule.* (n.d.). Stanford Registrar's Office, Stanford University. Retrieved from https://registrar.stanford.edu/students/tuition-and-fees (accessed 30 April 2016).

[99] Onink, Troy. (31 January 2015). *College costs could total as much as $334,000 in four years.* Forbes. http://www.forbes.com/sites/troyonink/2015/01/31/college-could-cost-as-much-as-334000-total-in-four-years/#371c686d679f

save for college and retirement. Yet, because they earn a relatively high income, getting need-based financial aid is not easy. While they may not be able to easily afford to write a check for $50,000 or more for a highly rated private university,[100] they are considered too wealthy to receive need-based aid. This is part of the all-too-familiar middle-class squeeze: too wealthy to directly benefit from government transfer payments and other subsidies, but not wealthy enough to have the worry-free life they aspire to have.

Overall, educating children is full of financial traps and tradeoffs that should be carefully considered. Whether it's paying for private elementary school or an out-of-state public college, parents who haven't yet funded their own level of financial freedom should consider the complete situation.[101] Carefully considering an outcome-based college education and targeting a four-year graduation pace makes solid financial sense. I try to be delicate about this latter point when talking with my clients. I ask: "What is the benefit of your being in your fifties and paying for a fifth year of college when you are already behind on your own goals?" It is important to remember that there is no guarantee that anyone will be able to continue working and earning into their 60s; so putting off your own retirement funding goals is a risky strategy. Unless you can afford it, try to avoid the trap of saying "yes" to paying for private elementary school, private high school, private college, extra years of college, and even some graduate school, if your own retirement plan isn't on track.

---

[100] *Trends in higher education: Average undergraduate prices by sector, 2015–2016.* (n.d.). College Board. Retrieved from http://trends.collegeboard.org/college-pricing/figure (accessed 28 June 2016).

[101] Davidson, Jacob. (18 August 2014). *How sending your child to private school can save you $53,000.* Money. Retrieved from http://time.com/money/3108717/private-school-public-school-costs/

A great example of flexible and prudent thinking comes from neighbors of mine whose son had his sights set on getting a degree from relatively expensive New York University. They were earning well over $200,000 per year but approaching age 60. The cost of college was an issue because they were significantly behind on their retirement goals. As a family, they carefully considered their options. They decided to send their son to a community college for his first two years to get some basic classes out of the way, and then transfer to NYU to focus on his major and finish his degree. This was not an easy decision for them to make, but they saved themselves well over $100,000 and the child's dream of graduating from NYU was realized. This is an example of careful planning that struck a smart balance.

There are other creative ways to get around the high cost of education. Comparing a few schools, working closely with a financial aid professional, and applying for a variety of scholarships can also help with the cost. A little thinking outside the box might help your kids receive the solid education you want them to have without your falling into middle-class poverty.

Summary: The Proactive Saver and Next Steps

The goal of this chapter has been to make the process of preparing for your retirement easier by sharing four of the behavioral traps that can get in your way. If you can develop a mindset that helps you avoid these traps, you will have a smoother journey to your financial freedom. One thing I have learned about people and their money is that just about everyone has at least some understanding of what they are doing financially. Those who look happy as they are freely spending large amounts of money may be, deep down, incredibly concerned about their financial future. Big spending can serve to mask fears, and it can be part of a spending trap that is difficult to stop.

My ultimate goal is to help you turn from being more *reactive* about your financial situation toward being more *proactive*. Why? Because the proactive saver usually has a far better chance of success. That's why, in this chapter, I talked about middle-class traps and how they stop us from saving. Hopefully, knowing the traps in advance will help you address them before you step into one or a number of them. In the next chapter, I will discuss becoming proactive around investing. If you are starting out on the road to accumulating wealth, or if you have a growing investment portfolio, I will share with you the enemies of the investor so that you can be a more informed investor.

CHAPTER 6

Avoiding the Four Enemies of the Investor: BITE

I've just covered four spending traps that confront the middle class, but there are also *investing* traps or "enemies of the investor" to avoid. I use the acronym BITE to remember the four big ones. They are as follows:

1. Bear Markets
2. Inflation
3. Taxes
4. Emotion

If you're not mindful of these enemies of the investor, they will *bite* you, taking a significant chunk of your financial security with them. Let's look more closely at what each one means, and more importantly, how to steer clear of them.

B = Bear Markets

Bear markets are perhaps the toughest enemy of the investor to avoid. The onset of a bear market is completely beyond the control of the individual investor. Typically, a bear market occurs when there is at least a 20% decline in broad-market index[102] prices over a period of two months or more.[103] *Market correction* is the term used when prices decline at a rate of 10% or more during a shorter time frame.[104] A market correction can kick off of a bear market. In a bear market, many people tend to get emotional and fearful about losses. They tend to want to sell their stocks, which is an attempt at *market timing*. This is a very difficult practice, even for the pros. Even if you do manage to sell at a good time, knowing when to get back in the market again isn't any easier. As Warren Buffett, one of the world's most well-known investors, has said, "It's harder to be right twice."

Bear markets are inevitable. They can also be prolonged, which can be particularly damaging to pre-retirees and retirees who still need their portfolios to grow. Reacting to a bear market can and often does end up being worse than the bear market itself; seeing the drop in portfolio value, an investor may pull out of the market and fail to get back in in time to benefit from a market recovery. One of the better ways to help you prepare for and respond to market declines is to structure your portfolio fully expecting that, at some point, risky investments like stocks will decline. And knowing your risk tolerance and building an appropriate portfolio consistent with your long-term goals may be a smart move in advance of any market decline.

Investors of a certain age will remember the prolonged bear market in the 1970s. The S&P 500 index, for example, peaked in

---

[102] Broad market index is an index designed to reflect the movement of the entire market.

[103] *What is a bear market?* (n.d.). Investopedia. Retrieved from http://www.investopedia.com/terms/b/bearmarket.asp (accessed 28 March 2016).

[104] *What is a Correction?* (n.d.). Investopedia. Retrieved from http://www.investopedia.com/terms/c/correction.asp (accessed 28 March 2016).

December of 1972 and closed at 118.05, but it plummeted to 63.54 by September of 1974.[105] The financial malaise was so widespread that individual and institutional investors alike began to fear that "stocks were never going to go up" again.[106] Prices stagnated for several years, and many investors changed their behavior in an attempt to time the market swings, while others pulled their money out altogether. But those who held fast eventually enjoyed good returns: the S&P 500 index improved from that low of 63.54 in September of 1974 to a high of 211.28 by the end of 1985.[107]

A painful bear market occurred after the collapse of the technology bubble in 2000. Then the stock market and world economy grew even worse after the September 11, 2001, terrorist attacks. The stock market continued its downturn into 2002.[108] During that time, the technology-focused NASDAQ[109] was significantly hit, falling from an all-time high of 5,049 on March 10, 2000,[110] to 1,114 on October

---

[105] *Interactive echarts.* (n.d.). Yahoo Finance. Retrieved from http://finance.yahoo.com/echarts?s=%5EGSPC+Interactive#{"customRangeStart":18000,"customRangeEnd":507618000,"range":"custom","allowChartStacking":true} (accessed 26 March 2016).

[106] Lauricella, Tom. (18 April 2009). *Flashbacks of the 1970s for stock-market vets.* The Wall Street Journal. Retrieved from http://www.wsj.com/articles/SB124001598168631027

[107] *Interactive echarts.* (n.d.). Yahoo Finance. Retrieved from http://finance.yahoo.com/echarts?s=%5Egspc+interactive#{"customRangeStart":18000,"customRangeEnd":504939600,"range":"custom","allowChartStacking":true} (accessed 26 March 2016).

[108] *Bear markets.* (n.d.). Wyatt Research. Retrieved from http://www.wyattresearch.com/markets/bear-markets/ (accessed 26 March 2016).

[109] The NASDAQ Composite Index is a market-valued, weighted index, which measures all securities listed on the NASDAQ stock market.

[110] Phillips, Matt. (2 March 2015). *The NASDAQ is back to its dot com bubble peak.* Quartz. Retrieved from http://qz.com/348954/the-nasdaq-is-back-to-its-dot-com-bubble-peak/

9, 2002,[111] constituting a 78% drop in 30 months! The damage was so severe (and compounded by the intervening financial crisis in 2007–2008) that the NASDAQ would not regain its March 2000 high until March 2015.[112]

Even investors who managed to avoid that bear market early in the first decade of the 2000s were largely caught unawares by the second one toward the end of that decade: a worldwide financial crisis that affected just about all equity investors. It was officially declared a bear market when the Dow Jones Industrial Average (DJIA)[113] fell from a high of 14,165 on October 9, 2007, to 11,216 on July 2, 2008,[114] losing more than 20% of its value in about nine months. The bear market persisted, causing the DJIA to continue to slip until finally bottoming out at 6,547 on March 9, 2009.[115] All told, the index lost 7,618 points over 18 months, or 54% of its peak value, and the more diversified S&P 500[116] lost even more (57%)![117]

---

[111] Glassman, James K. (11 February 2015). *3 lessons for investors from the tech bubble.* NASDAQ. Retrieved from http://www.nasdaq.com/article/3-lessons-for-investors-from-the-tech-bubble-cm443106

[112] McGugan, Ian, & Richard Blackwell. (2 March 2015). *A 15-year comeback: How Nasdaq regained its dot-com high.* The Globe and Mail. Retrieved from http://www.theglobeandmail.com/globe-investor/investment-ideas/how-nasdaq-regained-its-dot-com-high/article23245460/

[113] The DJIA is a widely followed measurement of the stock market. The average is comprised of 30 stocks that represent leading companies in major industries.

[114] *Interactive echarts.* (n.d.). Yahoo Finance. Retrieved from https://finance.yahoo.com/q/hp?s=%5EDJI+Historical+Prices (accessed 26 March 2016).

[115] Ibid.

[116] The Standard & Poor's 500 is an unmanaged group of securities considered to be representative of the stock market in general.

[117] *Interactive echarts.* (n.d.). Yahoo Finance. Retrieved from http://finance.yahoo.com/q/hp?s=^GSPC (accessed 26 March 2016).

While it's understandable that market declines can frighten an investor, the most important thing to know about a bear market is how to respond emotionally to it and not overreact at the wrong time. Markets have historically recovered from even the most devastating pullbacks. If you are prepared for the inevitable declines, you will deal with them better. However, if you invest so aggressively that you can't sleep well at night, or if you take on the very risky strategy of borrowing to buy stocks, your resulting declines can be traumatic. There's a reason people reportedly jumped out of windows on October 29, 1929, day one of the great stock market crash that is credited with leading us into the Great Depression. The S&P 500 fell a whopping 86% in less than three years and did not regain its previous peak for 25 years until 1954![118] This may explain why so many older investors never truly regained confidence in the stock market.

Hopefully, we'll never see such a severe depression again, but any bear market will reduce the amount of accumulated assets that you have invested in the stock market for your personal financial goals. That is why bear markets can have such a tremendous emotional impact on the investor. The often-cited Dalbar Quantitative Analysis of Investor Behavior (QAIB), commonly referred to as the Dalbar Study,[119] researches and reports on the returns of investors compared to benchmark indices over various periods of time. The 2015 QAIB report looks at 30 years of accumulated data on investor behavior. Its findings indicate that people make poor, and even irrational,

---

[118] *11 historic bear markets.* (n.d.). NBC News. Retrieved from http://www.nbcnews.com/id/37740147/ns/business-stocks_and_economy/t/historic-bear-markets/#.VdKzOc4nYqg (accessed 26 March 2016).

[119] *Qualitative analysis of investor behavior.* (n.d.). Dalbar. Retrieved from http://www.dalbar.com/ProductsampServices/AdvisorsSolutions/QAIB/tabid/214/Default.aspx (Last accessed 26 March 2016).

investment decisions based on emotional reactions. I'll talk more about reacting emotionally later in this chapter.

Bear markets in stocks are tough to handle at any age. The later in life they occur, the more likely they are to have undesirable consequences for investors with higher stock allocations. If you are nearing retirement age, you have fewer years to add to your investment portfolio and, quite possibly, a lower risk tolerance for riding the stock market roller coaster. One way to help avoid an emotional reaction is to build the right asset allocation for your risk profile before any market decline—so you are not tempted to change course during the downturn. The crux of the problem is that, even if you're a financial wizard, timing the highs and lows of the stock market is very difficult, and you can very easily end up selling low and buying high.[120] Selling low can lead to a permanent impairment of your capital, which is the outcome you most want to avoid.

This is where the guidance and benefit of a well-thought-out financial plan can have a positive impact. You should be having meaningful conversations with your financial adviser to discuss not just your investments, but also how you can better respond to the next bear market. The strategies you employ should be unique to you and your situation. And the closer you are to retirement, the more you should carefully consider your situation.

If you are a near retiree, you may want to look into whether you have reliable income sources that will protect you in the event of a prolonged bear market. This is where pensions and social security payments can be beneficial; with these two types of income sources, the amount of your monthly benefit is predetermined and increases

---

[120] Klein, Matthew C. (14 January 2013). *Irrationality, trend setting, and cats.* The Economist. Retrieved from http://www.economist.com/blogs/freeexchange/2013/01/investing

in accordance with cost of living adjustments. Your pension plan, provided it remains solvent and honors its promise, will not be affected by short-term stock market fluctuations. However, even pensions are not necessarily a sure thing. While the Pension Benefit Guaranty Corporation, a government agency, will guarantee most pensions, benefits beyond an annual payment of $60,136 are *not* guaranteed.[121] This means that if your private-sector employer goes bankrupt and succeeds in discharging its pension obligations, you may lose a sizeable portion of your planned retirement income.

But what if you have no pension?

If you don't have a pension, but the safety of a pension-like source of income is appealing to you, then look at fixed-income products offered by insurance companies. These products may offer a set amount of lifetime income guaranteed by the insurance company, so they may carry a little more certainty than traditional stock-and-bond portfolios. If these products appeal to you, you can select them in conjunction with your overall financial strategy and investment plan. If you do look into these products, select them very carefully as they can be very complex instruments and subject to a lot of restrictions.[122]

---

[121] *PBGC maximum insurance benefit level for 2015.* (27 October 2014). Pension Benefit Guaranty Corporation. Retrieved from http://www.pbgc.gov/news/press/releases/pr14-12.html

[122] Fixed annuities are usually long-term investment vehicles. Guarantees are subject to the claims-paying ability of the issuing insurance company. Early withdrawals, if withdrawn prior to age 59 1/2, may be subject to ordinary income tax, a 10% federal income-tax penalty, and contingent deferred sales charges.

What if you're young?

If you are in your 20s or 30s, you should pay little or no attention to bear markets. Why? Because you have time in the market to recover, time that a retiree or near retiree might not have. And remember, as the saying goes, "It's time in the market, not timing the market."

I = Inflation

Inflation is one of the most consistent and inevitable enemies of the individual investor. If, in an effort to try to avoid stock market losses associated with a bear market, you instead choose relatively lower-risk investments, you may experience a potentially lower return. A lower return may not provide you with what is known as a *positive real rate of return*. A positive real rate of return is a return greater than the rate of inflation.

The axiom that applies here is this: *the higher the risk, the higher the potential return; the lower the risk, the lower the potential return.* This is not a set rule, nor is it true in every case, but you can use this axiom as a general guideline for all investing. The lower the risk you take—which is a choice you may sometimes make in reaction to a bear market—the lower you can expect your return to be over the long term.

With today's low interest rates, lower-risk investments may have a rate of return that is sometimes as low as, or even lower than, the expected rate of inflation. If this is the case with one or more of the "safer" investments you've chosen, you must realize that while your investment may *feel* safe, it may actually be eroding your purchasing power, as it may carry a *negative real rate of return*. Even though inflation in recent years has been low by historical standards, an awareness of the impact of inflation may help guide you when making long-term investment decisions.[123]

Fortunately, social security has cost-of-living adjustments (COLA) to keep up with inflation. Not so, however, with personal investments. It is typically up to you to structure your personal investments in a way to help offset the inflation's impact. This usually means investing in risky assets in the hopes of growing above the rate of inflation. For example, let's look at a recently retired worker with an income need of $50,000 per year. With bank CD rates hovering in the 1% range, she has little choice but to move up the risk ladder to earn a higher yield. Otherwise, she will struggle to keep up with the rising prices that are inevitable with inflation. Remember, at 3% inflation, prices will double in 24 years. This means the assets generating income for this retiree will also need to grow in order to keep up with inflation. If they don't, inflation will ultimately lower her purchasing power.

As noted earlier, recent inflation rates have been historically low. But this doesn't eliminate inflation as a future threat. And, in the unlikely event that inflation stays low, it could well be the result of a slow economy, which has its own negative implications. A slow economy may tend to keep not only inflation but also interest rates low. The investment conundrum for an investor seeking safety will remain: how do you earn a positive real rate of return in a low-growth, low-inflation, and low-interest-rate environment? The answer, perhaps surprisingly, is the same for high-growth, high-inflation periods: take on as much prudent risk as you can tolerate so you can earn a positive real rate of return.

---

[123] *Current U.S. inflation rates 2006–2016.* (n.d.). US Inflation Calculator, CoinNews. Retrieved from http://www.usinflationcalculator.com/inflation/current-inflation-rates/ (accessed 26 March 2016).

T = Taxes

Two tax types to consider in relation to investments are ordinary income tax and the tax on dividends and capital gains. Typically, ordinary income is the higher of the two tax rates and is the tax rate that most people prefer to avoid. The government still allows favorable tax treatment on most dividends and on long-term capital gains.

What savers and investors may not know is that bank interest, such as CD and money market interest, is taxable as ordinary income for federal and state income tax purposes. Even other fixed-income investments, like corporate bonds and U.S. Treasury bonds, are subject to federal ordinary income taxes. In a period where rates of return are so low, this higher taxation category (ordinary income) can further reduce what is already a paltry rate of return on your interest income.

Ordinary income taxes, because they are typically such a high rate, can seriously reduce your ability to earn more than the inflation rate. This is true particularly for investors who choose lower-risk, fixed-income investments that are subject to ordinary income tax rates. Also subject to ordinary income tax rates are short-term capital gains, such as gains from short-term (less than one year) stock market investing. This is partly because the government, perhaps prudently, doesn't want to reward rapid trading and speculation. In fact, there is discussion of adding additional surtaxes on short-term trading activity.

For investors with a longer-term focus, which government policy aims to promote, there is a more favorable, but still painful, tax structure. Long-term capital gains and most dividends are also taxed, but usually at a favorable rate that varies based on your income level.[124] The current maximum, federal long-term capital gains tax rate is 20%; remember that your capital gains may also be subject to state income taxes and the 3.8% tax in the Patient Protection and Affordable Care Act.

Taxes on investments create a major headwind for all investors, but especially for younger investors who are trying to accumulate wealth. In this situation, you pay income tax on your earnings, and then you pay for living expenses and the taxes associated with daily life (e.g., sales taxes, gas taxes, and property taxes). If you are fortunate enough to then be able to save some money, the government might assess ordinary income tax on your interest income, or take anywhere from 20% to over 30% (state and federal combined) of any qualified dividends or long-term capital gains. For this reason, taxes are a major hurdle for young high-earners trying to reach their goal of financial independence or for those trying to accumulate enough assets to maintain even a middle-class lifestyle in retirement.

What might be even more painful to savers is that when they withdraw from their Individual Retirement Account (IRA), 401(k), and other retirement plans that were funded with pre-tax dollars, every dollar withdrawn is subject to ordinary income tax rates. There are no favorable tax rates for any growth inside these qualified retirement plans. For example, if you are a retiree who needs to take $20,000 from your 401(k), and your combined state and federal tax rate is 33%, then you will need to withdraw $30,000, $10,000 of which will go toward paying tax on your withdrawal. That $10,000 in taxes is a painful bite for most retirees.

There are some tax-smart strategies available, but the government continues to reduce tax-saving opportunities for the individual

---

[124] *Qualified dividends.* (n.d.). IRS. Retrieved from http://www.irs.gov/publications/p17/ch08.html#en_US_2014_publink1000171584 (accessed 26 March 2016).

investor. Because everyone's situation is different, careful and custom consideration should be given to your situation before trying to outsmart the taxman. Seek out a qualified Certified Public Accountant (CPA) or other tax professional to help with tax planning, and work with a Certified Financial Planner™ (CFP™) to strategize how to help mitigate the impacts of taxation on your investments.

E = Emotion

As the Dalbar study indicates, emotion is one of the biggest enemies of the investor. Intellectually, it's easy to understand that markets rise and fall. However, when you let emotion drive your decisions, you are taking a more short-term and short-sighted approach. When the market corrects with falling prices, you may have an emotional tendency to pull your investments out. This attempt to mitigate further damage to your investment portfolio by getting out of the market may be a misguided approach.

If you don't get back into the market in advance of the rebound, you may end up getting back in after a rebound at a higher price level. In this example, you would have sold low and bought higher, which is the exact opposite of what we all intend to do in order to achieve meaningful investment returns. Getting back into the stock market at a higher level results in what I call a "permanent impairment of capital," and that is when the mistake becomes real. Reactionary, emotional activity and decision making like this may eat away at your principal and make your recovery to previous portfolio levels take more time.

The real mistake in the 2007–2009 bear market wasn't being in the market as much as it was getting out of the market during the decline and not getting back in before the sharp reversal in prices. The market has risen substantially in the post-bear market between 2009 and 2016. The current bull market entered its eighth year in March of 2016 (becoming the second longest bull market in history). The Dow Jones Industrial Average (DJIA), for example, climbed almost 200% from a low of 6,469 to over 18,600 in mid-August 2016. [125] Though possible, it's unlikely that we're ever going to see those March 2009 lows again. So if you're one of those people who pulled out of the stock market, and you're waiting for it to go back down before you jump in again, consider that what you're doing is counterintuitive. You may actually be rooting *against* a strong economy and *for* a return to pre-crash-level stock prices. If you're waiting to return to stocks and sitting in cash, you are being penalized by an accommodative Fed, which continues to maintain a low-interest-rate policy.

Long-held emotional attitudes—some held since childhood, like playing it "safe" in cash—may result in decisions that leave significant returns on the table. Economics researcher Matthew C. Klein has even asserted that many investors are so irrational that they'd be better off letting a cat manage their money.[126] This partly explains why individual investors have underperformed the overall market time and time again.[127] Furthermore, we see that Millennials and younger Gen Xers who grew up with the twin bear markets of the 2000s tend to be lower-risk investors, despite their age. In this way, they resemble those who grew up and witnessed the devastation of the Great Depression.

So how can you avoid panicky, emotional reaction to events like a bear market? First of all, know your risk tolerance in advance.

---

[125] Dow Jones Industrial Average: Historical Prices. The Wall Street Journal. Retrieved from http://quotes.wsj.com/index/DJIA/historical-prices (accessed 25 August 2016).

[126] Klein, Matthew C. (14 January 2013). Irrationality, trend setting, and cats. The Economist. Retrieved from http://www.economist.com/blogs/freeexchange/2013/01/investing

[127] Seawright, Bob. (28 May 2014). *How advisors can make better investing decisions*. Research Magazine. Retrieved from http://www.thinkadvisor.com/2014/04/28/how-advisors-can-make-better-investing-decisions

Consider what your reaction might be to falling market values *before the markets inevitably decline.* Next, build a well-rounded, diversified portfolio that you can live with in both bull and bear markets. This can help keep your response to an inevitable decline less reactionary and more rational. Keep in mind that neither diversification nor asset allocation can guarantee against a loss; they are methods used to manage, not eliminate, risk.

This is where the guidance of an experienced financial adviser is essential. An experienced advisor can help you assess your investments and adjust your portfolio composition accordingly. If you feel you're taking too much risk, your advisor can help you switch into steadier, less volatile assets. Your financial advisor can be someone you can talk with when there is fear and panic swirling around.[128]

Summary

Any one of these BITE scenarios can have an adverse impact on your finances. None of us has any control over the coming and going of a bear market nor the rise and fall of inflation or tax rates. We can, however, make a plan and control our emotions. Consider the following:

- Mitigate the potential negative effects of a bear market, inflation, taxation, and emotion with long-term thinking.

- Build an investment portfolio fully knowing that stocks will decline, sometimes even severely.

---

[128] There are risks involved with investing, including possible loss of principal. Investments will fluctuate and may be worth more or less than when originally purchased. You should carefully consider your own investment objectives, risk tolerance, and time horizon before investing.

- Learn that losing money along the way is part of what happens to any successful long-term investor.

- Understand how inflation works and why it is not always best to play things too "safely."

- Benefit from asset allocation strategies whereby you locate your more tax-inefficient investments (like taxable bonds that carry ordinary-income-tax rates) into your tax-deferred accounts (like your IRA and 401(k)). In addition, stocks can be somewhat tax efficient even in a taxable account, and a lower-turnover stock portfolio might be more tax efficient than a very actively traded approach.

- Use a good tax advisor in conjunction with a knowledgeable Certified Financial Planner™ to strategize how to help mitigate the impacts of taxation on your investments. Final tax advice can be given only by a CPA or tax professional. It's hard to keep up with all the changes in tax law, let alone stay one step ahead of them, so turn to the experts.

- Temper your emotional reactions to market conditions. This is a tough one. You will need to be aware of your beliefs and attitudes about money. Some of our strongest beliefs develop from childhood. Much like those who grew up during the Depression, Millennials and Gen Xers who witnessed the stock market crashes of 2000 and 2008 will likely face emotional obstacles when deciding to invest in stocks. But it is important to manage your emotions. While there are no guarantees, for long-term investors, adding more risk may add more potential return.

CHAPTER 7

Avoiding the Financial Devastation of the Three Ds

Every day millions of Americans encounter one or more of the three Ds: divorce, disability, or the death of a parent, partner, or spouse. As we've seen, any one of these events can radically alter your financial situation and, by extension, your life. It's difficult if not impossible to completely prepare yourself emotionally for any of the three Ds. However, you *can* prepare for the potential financial impacts of these events. Preparing for catastrophic life events often makes it easier to manage their overall impact on your life. Let's look at each one thoroughly so you can understand their potential impact on your financial wellness and how best to address them.

Disability

The first D is for disability. Disabilities can occur over time or suddenly, but whether it's a poor health diagnosis or an unexpected accident, the daily financial struggle that results can be emotionally devastating and physically demanding. A disability creates stress and hardship and can turn your entire life routine upside down. Time spent working and enjoying hobbies will be replaced by hours of doctor visits and trips to specialists. The hassle of filing for benefits and completing and tracking all of the documentation demands by insurance companies and various entities adds an additional burden. This is not just a difficult time for the person with the disability; it also affects the entire family in many ways, often including a significant drop in household cash flow. Sadly, a portion of this financial struggle often can be avoided or at least mitigated.

Jack Smith (name fictionalized to protect privacy) and his wife were completely blindsided when Jack had to stop working for a six-month period due to an unexpected bout with cancer. Jack was self-employed and unable to work, so his income evaporated. He did not have a personal disability policy so he applied for social security disability benefits. Jack's application was rejected because his social security disability benefits did not kick in until after six full months of disability, and by then he had recovered. Fortunately, Jack was able to pay his bills during the months of treatment and recovery, but he had to spend down some of his hard-earned savings. He and his family struggled to replenish their retirement savings, and they learned some valuable lessons—namely that a personal disability policy could have provided valuable protection. Making things worse, now that Jack has been disabled, it will become even more difficult, if not impossible, for him to get his own disability income policy that could protect him in the future.

This situation underscores why it is important to apply for insurance early on, *before* you need the coverage. Once you have a bad diagnosis or have been seriously injured, your insurability is doubtful; insurance companies may see you as too big a risk.

Today's statistics on disability are alarming. According to the U.S. Social Security Administration, one-in-four of today's 20-year-olds will become disabled in their lifetime.[129] To be sure, many of them will make some sort of recovery and return to work, but the statistic points out a risk that is far too often overlooked by younger people who tend to eschew purchasing disability income protection.

Thirty-seven million, or about 12% of all Americans, are already disabled and currently receive some form of disability income. More than 50% of those who are disabled are in their working years, ages 18–64. According to the Social Security Administration, the number of Americans who are currently receiving some form of disability benefit has more than doubled since 1995.[130] Cynics may say that a lot of these claims are fake, but even if that is somewhat true, the reality is a lot of people legitimately file for disability benefits.

The Federal Old Age, Survivors, and Disability Insurance system was developed pursuant to the federal Social Security Act of 1935. In this legislation, the government instituted income protections for the disabled. However, these protections do not provide sufficient income benefits for today's middle-class workers to maintain their current lifestyle. Furthermore, about 65% of initial Social Security Disability Income (SSDI) claim applications were denied in 2012. This is not an easy process to go through as the possibilities of fraud lead to a diligent review, if not outright skepticism of claims. Adding to the difficulty, the threshold to receive social security disability benefits is quite high relative to a privately owned policy; so someone

---

[129] *Chances of disability: Me disabled?* (n.d.). Council for Disability Awareness. Retrieved from http://www.disabilitycanhappen.org/chances_disability/disability_stats.asp (accessed 22 June 2016).

[130] *Selected data from Social Security's disability program: Graphs of disabled worker data.* (June 2015). U.S. Social Security Administration. Retrieved from https://www.ssa.gov/oact/STATS/dibGraphs.html

would have to be in bad shape to even begin receiving social security disability benefits.

And even if you are *eventually* granted disability benefits, you will need to support yourself during the lengthy application process, which can take from six months to two years. Ninety percent of applicants report negative repercussions during the waiting period; this includes having to drain retirement savings (35%), missing making mortgage payments (14%), or being forced into filing for bankruptcy (5%).[131] Additionally, even if you're lucky enough to gain approval for SSDI payments, could you and your family live on the average disability payment of $1,165 per month? That was the average SSDI payment in 2015. I don't have to tell you it doesn't qualify as middle-class income in any of the 50 states.[132, 133] Some of the scariest statistics I've seen regarding disability are the following:

> Sixty-four percent of wage earners believe they have a 2% or less chance of being disabled for three months or more during their working career. However, for a worker who is entering the workforce today, the *real* odds are closer to 25%.[134]

---

[131] Allsup. (17 June 2013). *Disability applicants report facing foreclosure, lost health insurance, drained retirement savings and worsening illness.* Retrieved from http://www.disabled-world.com/disability/insurance/disability-applicants.php

[132] Kane, Libby & Andy Kiersz. (2 April 2015). *How much you have to earn to be considered middle class in every US state.* Business Insider. http://www.businessinsider.com/middle-class-in-every-us-state-2015-4

[133] Linebaugh, Melissa. (n.d.). *How Much in Social Security Disability Benefits Can You Get?* NOLO. Retrieved from
 http://www.nolo.com/legal-encyclopedia/how-much-social-security-disability-ssdi-benefits-can-you-get.html. (accessed 30 April 2016).

[134] *Disability Statistics.* (n.d.). Council for Disability Awareness. Retrieved from http://www.disabilitycanhappen.org/chances_disability/disability_stats.asp (accessed 22 June 2016).

> Most working Americans estimate that their chances of experiencing a long-term disability are substantially lower than the average worker's.[135]

Disability is, of course, a human tragedy that impacts people and families on a deeply personal level. But it is also a financial burden, and it is unfortunate how little people prepare for the financial aspect of this risk, which can often be at least somewhat mitigated. For example, 69% of workers in the private sector have no disability income insurance whatsoever.[136]

"Any Occupation" Versus "Own Occupation"

Even those employees whose companies offer disability insurance and find themselves covered under a large group policy, often don't know what protections they have. Benefits may be hard to understand, or they may not be as comprehensive as you actually need, so it is wise to take the time to better understand your coverage. For example, one major way that a group disability insurance policy can differ from a privately owned policy is the concept of "any occupation" versus "own occupation."

In a group policy, you will most likely find that the coverage is for "any occupation," which means that as long as you can perform any occupation at your company, then you are not considered disabled. Contrast that to some private policies that offer you the option of an

---

[135] *Disability divide: CDA 2010 consumer disability awareness survey.* (2010) Council for Disability Awareness. Retrieved from http://www.disabilitycanhappen.org/research/pdfs/ConsumerResearchReport_Consumer.pdf

[136] *Chances of disability: Me disabled?* (n.d.). Council for Disability Awareness. Retrieved from http://www.disabilitycanhappen.org/chances_disability/disability_stats.asp (accessed 22 June 2016).

"own-occupation" policy, meaning if you cannot perform the duties and responsibilities of your own, specific occupation, you qualify for benefits—even if you can still work in another occupation. This is the superior type of protection and the one that professionals, like physicians, usually request. After all, if a doctor specializing in surgery has a hand injury, that specialist does not want to be told he or she is not disabled because there is still the option to be a general practitioner.

Drawbacks to Group Disability Income Coverage

In addition to the weak definition of disability ("any occupation") there are several other drawbacks to a group policy, including potentially shorter benefit periods (many are only two years) and a lack of portability. "Lack of portability" means the coverage is in force only when you are employed and you cannot continue the coverage when you leave your employer. If you have health issues, this becomes very important as you are now left to hope that your next job comes with group disability insurance.

Another drawback to a group policy is that, if you already have group coverage, it might be difficult to get a privately owned policy. This is true regardless of how thin your coverage definitions might be. Insurance carriers don't want to over-insure an individual or create what is known as a "moral hazard." In this case, we are talking about the temptation for an able person to stop working and instead collect a large disability payment. But there are times, if you have a group policy, and you prefer to also have your own policy, that you can qualify for additional insurance. So talk with your insurance professional, who can try to get you additional coverage. For example, if you only have a two-year benefit period in your group plan, you might be able to find a carrier that will offer a policy with benefits that would start after the two years of your group coverage ends. For those who don't want to be left uninsured when they may need it most, a supplemental policy like this might be a sound strategy.

Who Should Own Their Own Disability Income Policy?

There are many variables to consider before purchasing income protection from a disability. If you are single, you might want the income to pay your bills and pay for some extra help around the house. When you are responsible for 100% of the household expenses, the need for coverage should be clear. If you are married or have a life partner and you are the major breadwinner in the household, you may have a lifestyle that your spouse cannot support. And, even in the event that you are not the main breadwinner in the family, your income may still be important, and your care might require additional expenditures. A disability income policy can help offset these expenses. Finally, if you have children, and you don't want their lives affected by your loss of income, a disability income policy can supplement your household cash flow. In some cases, you may need adaptive equipment or modifications to your home, and if you are now more dependent on your spouse and children for assistance around the house, you may need to deal with depression and the costs of psychological counseling. For all these reasons, the answer is that until you can self-fund a prolonged period of unemployment and still maintain adequate assets for your retirement, you should have a solid disability income policy. The one main caveat is that you need to have earned income in order to qualify for a policy. As valuable as being a homemaker is, the insurance protects your income from disability—if you are not earning wages, you cannot qualify for a policy.

I realize that disability insurance often seems expensive. If you are considering disability insurance, you are taking an admirable step toward protecting yourself and your family from a loss of income. But be warned, even if you are in the best of health, you might be disappointed at how much the coverage will cost. However, before you dismiss it over the cost, let's look at the importance and reasons behind the cost of disability insurance.

Let's say you are 34 years old and signing up for a disability insurance that will pay a benefit, after a 90-day waiting period, until you are age 65. If you file a claim nine months after issuance of your policy, your insurer could be on the hook for 30 years of monthly income payments. If your monthly disability benefit is $5,000, that equates to an obligation by the insurance company of $60,000 per year. In this case, over a 30-year period, the insurance company will be providing you with $1.8 million of income, plus possible cost-of-living adjustments (if included in your policy). That is a lot of (potentially tax-free) cash that you will receive! So while the cost of disability coverage is high, so is the benefit.

This hypothetical example underscores a huge point: the greatest financial asset a young person has is his or her future income. Knowing that your future income will likely be in the millions of dollars, why wouldn't you insure that? You will insure your home or car, and they will likely be worth far less. But younger people tend to think they are invincible or that disability won't ever happen to them—fortunately, for many of them, it won't. But if you are the one in eight Americans who become disabled with no coverage,[137] the impact on you and your family is going to be tremendous. On top of all the other personal struggles you are dealing with, you now have a financial calamity (that may have been avoidable with the proper coverage in place).

---

[137] Ibid.

While many of us can change our bad habits, or get in shape to reduce our chances of a disability, none of us can predict unforeseen accidents. You may be one of the eight million men or women who end up in the emergency room with a head trauma, broken bone, or disabling injury from a simple slip and fall. Long-term disability lasts 31.2 months, on average, so the financial impact can be devastating. Over half of all personal bankruptcies and mortgage foreclosures are a consequence of disability, according to a 2005 Harvard study.[138] It is very important to consider and prepare for these unforeseen accidents, but the financial burden can be prepared for, as well.

My job as a financial planner is not to *make* personal decisions for people, but rather to *explain* the financial ramifications of their decisions. To me, having adequate disability income insurance is perhaps one of the most important things any individual can do, at least until they can self-insure against any disability. I recommend having disability income insurance until you have an adequate amount of assets available not only to manage through a disability, but also to provide for a lifetime of retirement income. Most disability income policies have coverage limitations and will stop paying, usually at age 65 or age 67; so you need to think beyond this coverage period to consider how you will fund your retirement once disability income payments stop.

> I recommend having disability income insurance until you have an adequate amount of assets available not only to manage through a disability, but also to provide for a lifetime of retirement income.

And what amount of assets should someone have before they no longer need disability insurance coverage? That number will vary, but in many cases, it will mean having $1 million or more. Where

---

[138] Ibid.

do I get that number? Let's say you need $80,000 per year to live comfortably. To generate $80,000 of income in your first year of retirement, using a sustainable withdrawal percentage of 4% you would need $2,000,000 saved ($2,000,000 x 4% = $80,000). Therefore, until you have accumulated the targeted amount of assets that can provide income replacement for your financial freedom, you should consider the benefits of an insurance policy that protects your income against disability.

I haven't yet discussed the impact on your relationships when a disability hits. If you live in a household with someone who has a disability, whether it is a spouse or a dependent child, you are dealing with a lot of challenges. Disability income insurance can help reduce the financial stress your family will endure if you lose your income. If you suffer a long-term disability, how do you imagine the conversation will go with your spouse when she or he realizes you made the decision *not* to buy disability income insurance?

Not unexpectedly, divorce rates rise with a disability.[139] Divorce is the second of our three Ds, and it can also present significant economic implications to your life.

Divorce

Carol, the wife of an oil executive, got divorced shortly after her 60th birthday. It was her husband's decision to get the divorce, not hers. While married, she attempted to be the "good wife" and initially trusted he would treat her fairly in the divorce settlement. But things did not go as well as planned, and for the next 5 years, she spent a

---

[139] Hughes, Esquire, Barbara S. (n.d.). *When People with Disabilities Divorce.* Special Needs Alliance. http://www.specialneedsalliance.org/when-people-with-disabilities-divorce/ (accessed 22 June 2016).

significant amount of money on attorneys—enough to fund a good chunk of her retirement, had she been able to save it instead.

Carol didn't understand how much a divorce would impact her lifestyle, and in her rush to end the painful divorce process, she signed papers she didn't fully understand. After the divorce, she ended up spending money in ways she didn't realize would affect her retirement savings. Carol had married right out of college and had never focused on managing money or on her career. She didn't possess the right skills to get the kind of job that would afford her the luxuries she'd become accustomed to as the wife of an oil executive. Ultimately, Carol won enough of a settlement to support a middle-class life in Virginia. She learned to live on about one-quarter of what she had enjoyed living on while married. Carol had to learn about money from the ground up, never having previously bothered to understand how to create a spending plan or live within her means.

Of course, no one goes into a marriage or a domestic partnership thinking they will get divorced. The shift in income following a divorce is not something for which people usually plan. However, the financial impact on the spouses, especially women, can be significant. According to the Centers for Disease Control and Prevention (CDC), the rate of divorce in the U.S. approaches 50%.[140]

If you and your spouse argue about money, you're at a higher risk of divorce. In a 2012 study published in the journal *Family Relations*, researchers found that arguments about money *are*

---

[140] Miller, Claire Cain. (2 December 2014). *The divorce surge is over, but the myth lives on.* The Upshot, The New York Times. Retrieved from http://www.nytimes.com/2014/12/02/upshot/the-divorce-surge-is-over-but-the-myth-lives-on.html?abt=0002&abg=1

stronger predictors of divorce than any other type of argument.[141] / They further discovered that couples who argue about money early in their relationships—regardless of their income, debt, or net worth—are at a greater risk for divorce. Of course, it makes sense that fights about money impact a marriage. Oftentimes, couples argue about how to live on what they are making, or about the amount of debt they've incurred, or about how they are not funding an adequate retirement. The dissolution of a marriage, especially as people age, has a significant personal and familial component that can never be overlooked. As a financial advisor, I see the financial impacts of divorce far too often.

At all ages, divorce is often financially devastating for both partners. For young people who divorce, where there were once two incomes paying the rent and household expenses, there is now a need for each party to pay 100% of their own costs. During this difficult time, you need to make immediate adjustments, or the financial impact of your divorce will only get worse. For those who fail to adjust, consequences can be catastrophic. In 2010, 8% of the 1.5 million people who filed for bankruptcy cited a divorce as the leading cause.[142]

Older, affluent people who get divorced quickly learn how painful a split of assets can be. For example, if a household had $2 million to split equally in the divorce, it would result in each party getting $1 million. If we use our 4% sustainable withdrawal rate, this $1 million

---

[141] Dew, J., Britt, S. & Huston, S. (2012), *Examining the relationship between financial issues and divorce.* Family Relations 61: 615–628. doi: 10.1111/j.1741-3729.2012.00715.x, National Council on Family Relations.

[142] *Ten leading causes of bankruptcy.* (n.d.). Clear Bankruptcy. Retrieved from http://www.clearbankruptcy.com/financial-literacy/10-leading-causes-of-bankruptcy.aspx (accessed 28 June 2016).

generates about $40,000 in cash flow. While $1 million may seem like a lot of money, the income it can generate, in this case, puts you in the lower- to middle-class income range in most states.[143] If a non-working spouse receives $1 million before social security eligibility age, then he or she had better learn to live on about $40,000—or even less—if there are substantive changes to account value. Alternatively, it might make sense to earn extra income in order to avoid spending down principal at too rapid a pace.

Therefore, with this reduced income, on top of all the emotional travails of a divorce, you may have to cut out aspects of your life that you previously took for granted. For example, even an amicable divorce can affect your daily lifestyle, social networks, vacation plans, and goals for your children. A drop in income level will certainly change how often you can comfortably engage in the fun activities that would normally lift your spirits. Even if you are the higher-earning spouse who keeps your income and isn't required to pay alimony, it is reasonable to assume that approximately half of your accumulated marital assets will go to your spouse or partner in a divorce—and that you won't be able to replace them quickly.

So, to continue this scenario, your future retirement portfolio is now reduced by half, and it has to be replenished. If you are approaching retirement age, you will have only a few years to accumulate enough money to replace the portion that was split and in turn, to grow your savings from this adjusted lower amount. As you can see, after a divorce, other than for the very wealthy, it is difficult to maintain lifestyle and fund retirement without working longer or living more frugally. Alternatively, you can remarry a multimillionaire; but then,

---

[143] Kane, Libby & Andy Kiersz. (2 April 2015). *How much you have to earn to be considered middle class in every US state.* Business Insider. http://www.businessinsider.com/middle-class-in-every-us-state-2015-4

of course, there is the looming possibility of the dreaded prenuptial agreement!

Death

Death is often the most difficult personal and familial tragedy we experience. It's also often unexpected, especially if the person who has passed is young or seemingly healthy at the peak of his or her earning potential. As I mentioned in chapter 1, Patti Morton—the former Dallas Cowboys marketing manager and the widow of the former CompUSA CEO, Nathan Morton—learned it's never too soon to prepare for the unexpected. Patti was married to Nathan Morton for less than five years when he suddenly died of a heart attack during a bout with pneumonia. "It was so sudden, so unexpected," said Patti. "And all I could think was, 'We didn't have enough time, we didn't have enough time.'"

In the two years under Nathan Morton's leadership, CompUSA grew to over $2 billion in revenues. Morton also partnered with Apple in creating the "store within a store" concept to sell Apple computers inside a megastore. By January 1998, CompUSA had built 57 stores to sell Apple and other products. Morton left CompUSA in 1993 to pursue other businesses, including starting his own company, which was due to launch on the London Stock Exchange. However, just 17 days prior to this initial public offering, he suddenly died. Unfortunately for Patti, not only did she deal with the grief of losing her husband, the public launch never happened, and so neither did the expected financial influx.

According to Patti, "Nathan had a lot of things going on." Here's how she explained it:

"He made some investments right before the dot-com bubble burst—putting us a million dollars into debt. He was preparing to launch a new venture, one that would have been very lucrative, and he just never got around to planning our financial future. His first wife received a substantial life insurance settlement as per a prior divorce agreement. So she was taken care of. But the insurance settlement I received was very small and not nearly enough to consider living on, let alone retiring on."

After her husband's death, Patti said she also became a victim to people who prey on widows with money. She ended up being scammed out of what money she had received, plus her home and car. She lost almost everything and was left to rebuild from almost nothing. However, she persevered, developed her skills, and built her own career. Patti is now a successful marketing executive and has worked hard to make back the money she lost. Unfortunately, not everyone is able to rebuild financially the way Patti did, and that is why early planning is so important.

Like disability, death of a partner is something for which you can financially prepare. Fortunately, unlike disability income insurance, term-life insurance is relatively inexpensive (because the level premium period is only for a set number of years). For example, if you're a healthy female in your late 30s who qualifies for a preferred rating, you may get a 20-year level premium term life insurance policy with a death benefit of $900,000 for about $50 per month.

A typical middle-class couple in their mid-30s may be looking at $2 million to $5 million (and perhaps more, if you consider pay increases) of lost income if the primary breadwinner passes away. Plus, the family can experience a huge emotional disruption, regardless of whether a wage earner or non-working spouse dies. Without adequate income-generating assets that life insurance can provide, the surviving spouse may have to go back to work instead of staying home with children. This may also add the cost of childcare to an already unfortunate situation.

From a financial planning standpoint, I counsel my clients that protecting one's family should be a part of almost every young parent's financial plan. This means even a non-working spouse needs life insurance. In cases where there is a primary breadwinner, I've seen many couples struggle with being underinsured because they're insuring only the working spouse. The best way to avoid being underinsured is to provide adequate insurance for both spouses, no matter who is bringing home the lion's share of the income. The logic, especially with men, is this: *Well, I'll go back to work and continue to earn my salary, so why do I need life insurance on my wife when I make most of the money?*

In these situations, I try to find a way to gently ask, "Really? After your wife dies, you're still going to leave early in the morning five days a week, power through your full day, and meet your kids in time to facilitate afternoon and evening activities including providing dinner?" Usually, the response I get to these discussions is an uncomfortable silence. The reluctance to plan for a potential death in the family is understandable, because death is such a difficult topic. But there also seems to be reluctance in some situations to fully appreciate the economic value that both parents play. The fact is that both parents need to be adequately insured, and unless there is a health or underwriting issue, a middle-class family should seriously consider protecting their family with term life insurance.

As with disability insurance, life insurance coverage should remain in place until you have achieved some level of assets that can self-fund your life goals (including college and retirement). Of course, there are various types of life insurance, but for the purposes of protecting a young family, term life insurance is a solid start and can help the survivors avoid middle-class poverty. I have personally seen the benefit life insurance played in real people's lives. The few "death checks" from insurance companies that I have delivered to widows have dramatically improved the lives of the children in those families. For the relatively small amount of money term life insurance costs, you could take a major worry entirely off the table. And, how often in life do any of us get the chance to do that?

Summary

- Be aware of the three Ds and their potential catastrophic impacts.

- If you are of pre-retirement age, consider getting a disability income insurance plan.

- Talk about money with your partner or spouse, and take the time to sit down and discuss what life might be like if one of you were unable to work. This can be done as part of your written financial plan.

- Share your attitudes and beliefs about money with your spouse or partner as you begin to plan a life together.

- As partners, once you have insights into the "why" behind your individual behaviors, you'll better understand the issues behind each other's spending decisions. You may even be able to agree on making changes that will enable you both to feel more comfortable with your current situation. Moving forward together with a plan is a great way to solidify your relationship by working as a team.

- Your ultimate goal should be for both you and your spouse to become financially literate. Be continuously aware and knowledgeable about your financial plan and all of your assets. Continue to educate yourself about financial matters, even if your partner handles your finances.

- In the event of a divorce, try to keep a calm and loving mindset before it ever becomes a heated, emotionally charged issue. When there are substantial assets on the table, legal fees in contentious divorces can easily exceed $100,000 or more.

- Make investment decisions jointly. Don't blindly let one spouse make all the decisions. When only one spouse is handling the financial planning and that spouse dies, the surviving spouse is often left unprepared and uninformed on how to proceed with the financial care of themselves and the family.

- Review your financial plan, in the event the primary earner passes away. Run income projections with your assets and existing life insurance. If there is a shortfall, take corrective action. Usually, this means adding or increasing life insurance coverage.

- Visit your financial planner at least once a year to review your specific risks based on any of these three Ds.

CHAPTER 8

401 Not OK

Since its inception in 1978, the 401(k) retirement plan has become the most recognized and popular type of employer-sponsored retirement plan in America. With the demise of the pension system in the United States, millions of workers now depend on the money that they have saved in their 401(k) plans to provide for their retirement.[144] The 401(k) retirement plan is a popular employee benefit because employees can use the plans to put pre-tax compensation, up to the IRS limit, into retirement savings accounts. And, if your employer chooses to match all or a portion of what you contribute into your plan, then the advantages of your 401(k) plan are enhanced.[145]

When the 401(k) was initially created, it was meant to complement pension plans that, along with social security, provided retirement income for millions. It was not designed to replace valuable pensions. However, one of the plan's unintended consequences was that many companies stopped offering their employees pensions and started

---

[144] *Why 401(k)s are the most popular employee retirement plan benefit and how they work.* (13 January 2014). BizFilings. Retrieved from http://www.bizfilings.com/toolkit/sbg/office-hr/managing-the-workplace/401k-employee-retirement-plan.aspx

[145] Ibid.

offering 401(k) plans instead. Pensions had been popular in corporate America for many years and may have a longer history than you might imagine.

The first pension plans were started by the Romans over 2,000 years ago. Later, the Continental Congress used them during the American Revolution as a way to entice men to join General Washington's fight against the British army. The incentive was a lifetime income if they fought in and survived the war. We repeated the offer during the Civil War, and still to this day, we justifiably reward our honorable veterans with a lifetime income payout.

The first private pension plans appeared in 1875 when American Express established pension accounts for its workers. Soon other companies and governments followed. In 1883, Chancellor Otto Von Bismarck of Germany had a problem. Marxists were threatening to take control of Europe. To help his countrymen resist their blandishments, Bismarck announced that he would pay a pension to any non-working German over the age of 65. Bismarck was no dummy. Not many people lived to be 65 at the time. Bismarck not only co-opted the Marxists, but he also set the arbitrary world standard for the exact year at which old age begins—establishing the precedent that government should pay people for growing old.[146] We now have life expectancies well beyond 65, but our pension and social security systems have not adapted. As a result of longer life expectancies, pension costs have risen dramatically, which has contributed to pensions becoming increasingly rare. For the same reasons, Social Security is also struggling financially.

---

[146] Weisman, Mary-Lou. (21 March 1999). *The history of retirement, from early man to A.A.R.P.* The New York Times. Retrieved from http://www.nytimes.com/1999/03/21/jobs/the-history-of-retirement-from-early-man-to-aarp.html

The Decline of Pensions in America

In America, workers loved the lifetime income benefit that pensions provided, and it also gave employers more loyal workers. Pensions were beloved—as long as the employer didn't go bankrupt and break its promises. In 1974, after several high-profile company failures that left some workers receiving little or none of their promised benefits, the government created the Pension Benefit Guaranty Corporation (PBGC) to guarantee a portion of the promised pension if the company were to go out of business.

Like many government responses, the creation of the PBGC was well intentioned and addressed a growing problem. However, it also raised the cost of running a company pension plan. New government scrutiny led to additional reporting responsibilities and administrative fees for companies. And when the costs of carrying a pension rose, pensions became less attractive to corporate boards of directors. The result was the continued decline of a pension system already burdened by longer life expectancies and erratic investment markets.

Later, in 2006, the Pension Protection Act (PPA) was passed. It was designed to safeguard pensions from budget shortfalls by requiring companies to guarantee that plans were nearly or completely funded. However, the PPA may have accelerated the demise of the pension as the new rules triggered a "significant acceleration in the pace of plan freezes," at least according to findings by the Employee Benefit Research Institute (EBRI) and Mercer Human Resources Consulting. According to this study, with the risks of investing falling on the plan sponsor (the employer), many employers began closing traditional pension plans. Employers instead focused on increasing their contributions to traditional 401(k) plans, where the investment risk falls on the employee (not on the employer).[147]

With the growing popularity and acceptance of 401(k) plans, many companies decided to replace costly defined benefit pension plans with defined contribution plans, like a 401(k) plan. The shift was not the result the government intended when it offered workers a way to invest some of their earnings on a pre-tax basis. However, the marketplace has its own way of finding efficiencies and lowering costs. In this case, many workers in a wide range of income levels wound up working for companies that no longer offered pension plans, as you can see in the chart below.

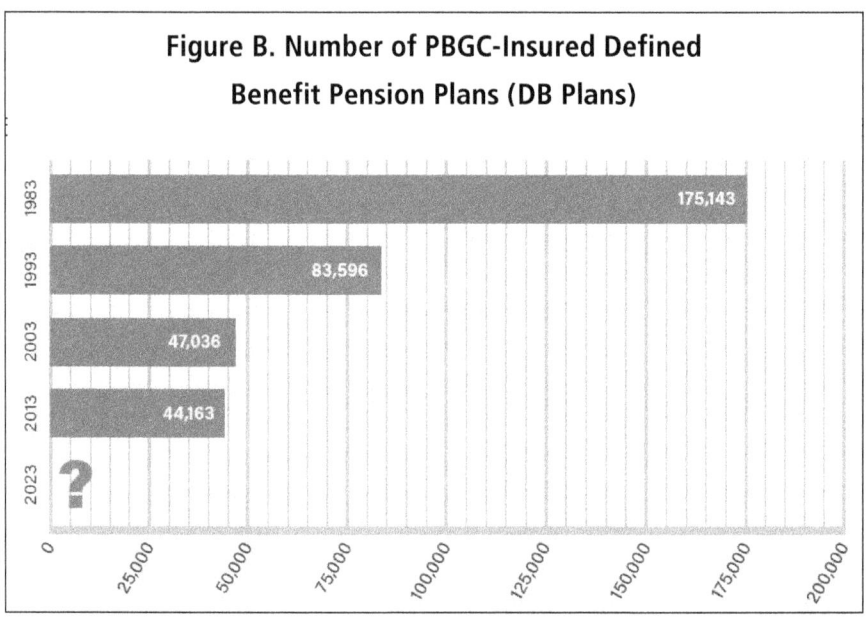

Source: U.S. Department of Labor Private Pension Plan Bulletin Historical Tables and Graphs 1975-2013, Report Issued September 2015

---

[147] *Pensions decline as 401(k) plans multiply.* (n.d.). Bankrate. Retrieved from http://www.bankrate.com/finance/retirement/pensions-decline-as-401-k-plans-multiply-1.aspx#ixzz3qVxnfyHv (accessed 22 June 2016).

As Bob Dylan said, "You don't need a weatherman to know which way the wind blows." And on this one, it is clear that pensions are on a decline toward near extinction. So if you have a pension, especially if it contains cost-of-living adjustments, you are one of the fortunate. Other than any pensions, social security, or an inheritance, you will need to save in order to create your own retirement income.

The shift from pensions to 401(k) plans was one of the biggest shifts in employer-employee relations in our country's history, yet many people still do not fully understand its impact. At the least, the educational piece has fallen short, leaving tens of millions of Americans underprepared for their retirement. And this lack of preparation is not just among lower earners. Higher earners need to save even more if they want to avoid a dramatic reduction in their standard of living.

> Higher earners need to save even more if they want to avoid a dramatic reduction in their standard of living.

This is why I emphasize financial education and a commitment to pursuing the goals of your written financial plan. Included in your plan should be a monthly cash-flow worksheet that can help you determine an amount available for automatic savings. Automatically having money taken out of your paycheck for saving helps avoid the temptation to spend this amount. This is one of the advantages of a 401(k) plan: it allows you to automatically invest a portion of your earned income before it hits your checking account.

The Shift to Defined Contribution Plans

As popular as they are, 401(k) plans were never designed to be the sole source of your retirement income. They were created to give you another source of income in addition to your savings, pension, social security benefits, and other retirement income.[148] Unfortunately for workers, many private companies and even the federal government have abandoned their traditional pension plans, also known as *defined benefit plans*.

They are called *defined benefit plans* because the benefits are defined by a formula set by plan actuaries. According to the U.S. Labor Department, as recent as the early 1980s, 85% of full-time workers at large companies and 35% of all private workers were covered by a defined benefit plan. But by 2011, that dropped to 18% for all workers.[149] In a pension plan, the worker does not contribute to the plan; only the employer contributes. This means the employer also makes all the investment decisions, which brings the employer added costs and risks. These pensions have largely been replaced by 401(k) plans, 403(b) plans, and Thrift Savings Plans (TSPs), which are all called *defined contribution plans*. TSPs and 403(b) plans are similar to 401(k) plans but are for federal and state employees and employees of not-for-profit entities. For simplicity, I am using the term "401(k)" for all defined contribution plans. In 401(k) plans, the participant makes the investment decisions, even if they have no investment experience.

---

[148] Guina, Ryan. (15 March 2011). *5 reasons your 401K isn't enough for retirement.* U.S. News & World Report. Retrieved from http://money.usnews.com/money/blogs/on-retirement/2011/03/15/5-reasons-your-401k-isnt-enough-for-retirement

[149] Wiatrowski, William J. (December 2012). *The last private industry pension plans: A visual essay.* Monthly Labor Review, U.S. Bureau of Labor Statistics, U.S. Department of Labor. Retrieved from http://www.bls.gov/opub/mlr/2012/12/art1full.pdf

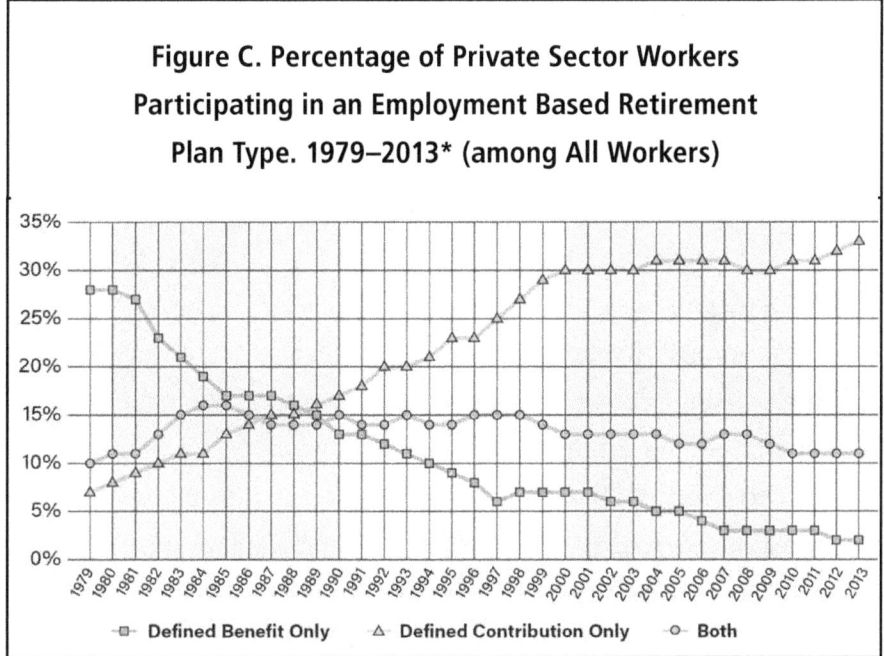

SOURCE: U.S. Department of Labor Form 5500 Summaries 1979-1998. Pension Benefit Guaranty Corporation. Current Population Survey 1999-2011. EBRI estimates 1999-2010.

Defined contribution means that only the contributed amount is defined, and the benefit is not certain. Therefore, the benefit that each person receives in a defined contribution plan is unknown. In other words, there is no guaranteed lifetime income received by a participant of a defined contribution plan, such as a 401(k). This differs from pension plans, in which the lifetime income amount is known—assuming the plan sponsor remains solvent. See Figure 1 for changes over time in several types of employment-based retirement plans.

There are many reasons for the shift away from pensions, but costs are near the top of the list. The main driver of the cost increases is lengthening life expectancies. These increases are also one of the main reasons for social security's financial struggles. In 1935, when

Social Security started, the average life expectancy was 61.7 years.[150] By 2013, life expectancies had risen to 78.8 years—a difference of more than a decade and a half. This means the length of time social security has to continue to pay the average individual is far more than when the program started. This is one reason that social security taxes have risen significantly over the years, yet the program is still under financial stress.

These longer life expectancies also mean that companies still offering pension plans must set aside more money to cover a longer benefit period. As America's corporate landscape has changed in reaction to more global competition, cost cutting has become an important way to maintain market share. Pension plans have not been as widely offered outside the US, so in an effort to stay competitive, American companies have downsized or eliminated their pension plans.

Limits and Shortfalls of Defined Contribution 401(k) Plans

I believe this decline in pension plans has been accompanied by the failure of corporations and the government in two key areas: (1) educating the workforce, and (2) IRS limits on pre-tax contributions into 401(k) plans.[151]

Regarding education, I do not think the public was aware of the seismic shift that was happening with their retirement plans when

---

[150] Arias, Elizabeth. (6 November 2014). *United States life tables, 2010.* National Vital Statistics Reports, (vol 63, no 7.) National Center for Health Statistics, CDC. Retrieved from http://www.cdc.gov/nchs/data/nvsr/nvsr63/nvsr63_07.pdf

[151] Morrissey, Monique. (11 January 2013). *Private sector pension coverage.* Economic Policy Institute (EPI) [Blog]. Retrieved from http://www.epi.org/blog/private-sector-pension-coverage-decline/

pension plans were replaced by 401(k) plans. Low-wage workers, who were significantly impacted by the change, often lacked financial education and did not have the excess cash flow to adequately self-fund their retirement. Sure, there was required communication, but this need to self-fund retirement was a new, complex concept to many and merited greater emphasis on bringing workers up to speed. Looking at the current, low amount of accumulated savings among a majority of Americans, it's easy to see the failures brought about by a shift to defined contribution plans.

The retirement savings shortfalls are not just among lower-income workers. I meet many highly educated, higher earners who don't fully grasp the extent of their retirement savings challenge. Making the situation worse, 401(k) employee salary deferral (contribution) limits, in my opinion, have been set too low to adequately fund most middle-class and affluent retirements.

The government limits 401(k) plan pre-tax employee contributions, as demonstrated in the following table:

Table C. Maximum Allowed, Pre-tax Employee Contribution into 401(k)

YEAR	MAXIMUM AMOUNT OF PRE-TAX EMPLOYEE CONTRIBUTION
1987	$ 7,000
1997	$ 9,500
2007	$15,500
2016	$18,000

Source: Department of Labor, Potomac Wealth Advisors, LLC

These limits often have an unintended, adverse effect, as many people think that by contributing an amount close to the maximum allowable 401(k) contribution they are adequately saving for retirement.

When the federal government limited 401(k) contributions (perhaps in the interest of limiting pre-tax contributions and maintaining tax revenue), they set a low bar for savers. The limit was not designed to result in a specific amount of retirement income. Savers should know that the maximum allowable IRS contribution has no relevance to their unique financial plan. And we are now seeing the disappointing results as the first generation of 401(k) workers retires.

Most 401(k) plans also impose a great deal of rules and regulations on both the sponsoring company and individual investor. Sure, some regulations are designed to help and protect workers, but they come at a cost and with great complexity. The regulations can be a disincentive to employers when it comes to offering a plan. Business owners who offer plans take on serious fiduciary responsibilities, which lead many small businesses to forgo offering any plan. For those companies offering plans, an increase in the maximum contribution limit would help workers interested in saving. There was some progress made on raising this limit when the "catch-up contribution" was added, but this was only a small step toward recognizing and fixing the problem. Overall, 401(k) plans need to be more robust for savers and friendlier to plan sponsors.

The Catch-Up Provision

A *catch-up contribution* is a type of retirement savings contribution that allows people over age 50 to make additional contributions to their 401(k) and/or individual retirement accounts. The catch-up contribution provision was created by the Economic Growth and Tax Relief Reconciliation Act of 2001 (EGTRRA) so that older individuals would be able to set aside enough savings for retirement.[152] If you are

---

[152] *Retirement topics: Catch up contribution.* (n.d.). IRS. Retrieved from http://www.irs.gov/Retirement-Plans/Plan-Participant,-Employee/Retirement-Topics-Catch-Up-Contributions (accessed 22 June 2016).

50 or older, it is a way for you to try to "catch up" if you have not yet put enough funds toward your retirement goals.

Adding the catch-up provision was a small acknowledgement by Congress that we had a looming retirement planning crisis in our country. However, they only created the catch-up contribution for workers 50 years of age or older, probably because they wanted a smaller revenue hit to the U.S. Treasury. Workers 50 years of age, or older, will tend to withdraw funds from their 401(k) plans sooner than younger workers. Older workers have less time for these assets to benefit from the power of compounding, and as I will discuss later, 401(k) plans are tax inefficient for a retiree who withdraws from them. These two factors can make the contributions into a 401(k) plan less valuable for older workers than those of younger investors, yet older workers are the ones eligible for the catch-up provision.

The Challenge for Plan Providers and Investors

As I mentioned previously, in addition to relatively low deferral limits, 401(k) plans carry a lot of rules and regulations. For example, employers who offer plans are fiduciaries. A *fiduciary* is a person or institution given the power to act on behalf of another in situations that require great trust, honesty, and loyalty. Fiduciaries of 401(k) plans face severe penalties if they do not administer their plans appropriately. This is one reason many small and mid-size companies choose not to offer a plan. If they do offer a 401(k) plan, they persevere through time-consuming responsibilities, complexities, and costs, which many pass on to the plan participants. Meanwhile, these plan costs have caught the eye of government regulators who press the financial service industry for lower fees. We can debate to what extent both sides make good points, and the government certainly has a basis for wanting lower 401(k) plan costs for all participants, but one of the best ways to do this, especially for these smaller plans, would be to streamline regulations.

Perhaps the bigger issue isn't what is happening inside these plans, but what is not happening for the many workers who don't participate in a plan. In a 2014 Bureau of Labor Statistics report, just 53% of American workers reported participating in any type of retirement plan at work.[153]

With all the economic headwinds I have discussed, including stagnant wages, underemployment, an increasing cost of living, and higher taxes, it is easy to see why this current generation of workers is saving less than needed. Factor in the higher costs of health insurance, higher deductibles, and higher co-pays, and it's even clearer why employees with 401(k) plans are seriously underfunding them.[154] According to an Employee Benefit Research Institute (EBRI) and Greenwald and Associates survey, about 36% of workers have less than $1,000 in savings and investments that could be used for retirement, not counting their primary residence or defined benefits plans such as traditional pensions. And 60% of workers have saved less than $25,000 for retirement.[155]

According to *"How America Saves,"* a yearly publication produced by Vanguard where it surveys participants in its retirement plans, the

---

[153] Vernon, Steve. (27 October 2014). *Half of Americans aren't in a retirement plan*. CBS MoneyWatch, CBS News. Retrieved from http://www.cbsnews.com/news/half-of-all-american-workers-not-covered-by-a-retirement-plan/

[154] MacDonald, John A. (July 2006). *The employment-based pension system: Evolution or revolution?* Employee Benefit Research Institute. Retrieved from https://www.ebri.org/pdf/notespdf/EBRI_Notes_07-20061.pdf

[155] Helman, Ruth, Adams, Nevin, J.D., Copeland, Craig, & Jack VanDerhei. (March 2014). *The 2014 retirement confidence survey: Confidence rebounds—for those with retirement plans*. Issue Brief (no 397), Employee Benefit Research Institute. Retrieved from https://www.ebri.org/pdf/briefspdf/ebri_ib_397_mar14.rcs.pdf

median employee savings rate was 6%, and only 22% of participants contributed more than 10% of their pay to a 401(k), let alone saving the maximum.[156] Many middle-income and even high-income earners I have met think that by contributing, or even "maxing out," their 401(k) plan, they are on the road to a successful retirement. I don't know where that mindset started, but it seems to be somewhat rooted in magical thinking. Do we *really* think the IRS maximum-allowed-amount was designed with a person's financial success in mind?

The most cited reason for the underfunding of retirement plans is the cost of day-to-day expenses that leads to a lack of savings. This is why pensions are so beneficial to workers. Even if the employee contributes nothing, a pension can still provide them lifetime income throughout retirement. Workers covet their pensions, and that helps create an unwritten social contract whereby workers usually stay at the same company for most of their careers in return for retirement security.[157]

The decline of pensions contributes to workers being less loyal to their employers. But changing jobs further strains a worker's ability to fund 401(k) plans that often have waiting periods for eligibility. The average worker stays at a job 4.4 years. According to the Future Workplace Multiple Generations at Work (GAO) survey of 1,189 employees and 150 managers, 91% of Millennials (born from 1977–1997) expect to stay in a job for less than three years.[158] Changing jobs not only ends any additional

---

[156] King, Martha. (June 2015). *How America saves: A report on Vanguard 2014 defined contribution plan data.* Vanguard. Retrieved from https://institutional.vanguard.com/iam/pdf/HAS15.pdf

[157] *Pre-Social Security period: Traditional sources of economic security.* (n.d.). Social Security Administration. Retrieved from http://www.ssa.gov/history/briefhistory3.html (accessed 17 January 2016).

[158] *Multiple generations at work: Five generations working side by side in 2020.* (n.d.). Future Workplace. Retrieved from http://futureworkplace.com/wp-content/uploads/MultipleGenAtWork_infographic.pdf (accessed 17 January 2016).

pension benefit accrual that would have accumulated with the former employer, it starts a new eligibility clock with the new company's 401(k) or pension plan.[159] Even if your new company has a 401(k) plan, you may still miss up to a year or longer if there is a restrictive entry policy.

We now live in a world where, other than social security income, most people handle their own retirement income planning. Yet as we just saw, many do not contribute enough to adequately fund their retirement plans. In fact, it is only the wealthiest 20% of American households that even have, on average, more than one year's income accumulated in these accounts,[160] and that is still not nearly enough. Even worse, about 29% of households with workers age 55 or older have no retirement savings, according to a GAO study. Among those with some retirement savings, the median amount of those savings is about $104,000 for households with earners age 55–64 and $148,000 for earners age 65–74.[161] If we use our 4% sustainable withdrawal rate on these amounts, we can see that this generates an income below federal poverty-level guidelines, which is why so many people end up relying almost solely on social security for their retirement income.

Maxing Out Your 401(k) May Still Not Be Enough

"Even if a middle-income worker embraces their 401(k) plan," according to a study from the Economic Policy Institute, "a 401(k)

---

[159] *FAQs about retirement plans and ERISA*. (n.d.). U.S. Department of Labor. Retrieved from http://www.dol.gov/ebsa/faqs/faq_consumer_pension.html (accessed 19 June 2016).

[160] Holland, Kelley. (23 March 2015). *For millions, 401(k) plans have fallen short*. CNBC. Retrieved from http://www.cnbc.com/2015/03/20/l-it-the-401k-is-a-failure.html

[161] Parker, Tim. (n.d.). *The average retirement savings by age for 2016*. Investopedia. Retrieved from http://www.investopedia.com/articles/personal-finance/011216/average-retirement-savings-age-2016.asp (accessed 21 April 2016).

plan by itself is not going to provide sufficient returns for a meaningful retirement."[162] This might be one of the most important statements that should be repeated over and over again to everyone working toward their financial freedom. It should be as familiar to all of us as the warnings about cigarettes. We are looking at a social crisis in our country in the coming decades, and it stems in part from a lack of awareness.

As I discussed earlier, abject poverty is by far the greater tragedy, but the societal impact of underfunded retirements and pending middle-class poverty will also be felt throughout our country. Economic vitality and opportunity will be stifled with a trickle-down effect throughout all social strata. This is why, as a nation, we need to educate everyone on the need and importance of saving. As a nation, we talk about the dangers of smoking, childhood obesity, high fat diets, global warming, and other issues. But we don't reinforce, educate, or promote financial independence, and people need to know more about the challenge ahead.

How Much Will Be Enough?

It may be helpful to demonstrate what saving the current IRS 401(k) maximum can lead to in real terms for a younger worker, 30 years away from retirement:

> Let's say you save the 2016 IRS annual maximum ($18,000)[163] by making contributions of $1,500 each

---

[162] Von Hoffman, Constantine. (4 September 2013). *Study: 401(k) retirement plans failing most workers*. CBS MoneyWatch, CBS News. Retrieved from http://www.cbsnews.com/news/study-401k-retirement-plans-failing-most-workers/

[163] *IRS announces 2015 pension plan limitations: Taxpayers may contribute up to $18,000 to their 401(k) plans in 2015*. (23 October 2014). IR-2014-99. IRS. Retrieved from http://www.irs.gov/uac/Newsroom/IRS-Announces-2015-Pension-Plan-Limitations-1

month—and you do this for 30 years. If we estimate a 7% compound annual growth rate, the ending balance of your savings will accumulate to approximately $1,830,000. And this amount, which approaches almost two million dollars, may seem like a lot of money. But let's take a closer look at what this means after adjusting for inflation.

Using the same IRS annual maximum ($18,000)[164] invested through $1,500 monthly contributions for 30 years, and if we estimate a 7% compound annual growth rate and include a 3% estimated annual inflation rate, the net growth on your contributions is reduced to 4% per year. This 4% is known as the *real rate of return* (the rate of return after adjusting for inflation). Based on these assumptions, your saving results in a balance, in real terms, of $1,040,000. This may still seem like a lot of money—and for some it certainly is.

But using our 4% sustainable withdrawal rate, your retirement will start with an annual pre-tax retirement cash flow of $41,600. While $41,600 is nothing to sneeze at, someone who was able to save $18,000 per year probably had a gross income significantly higher than $41,600. The Economic Policy Institute is correct: saving the IRS maximum 401(k) amount is probably not going to be enough to maintain your lifestyle. Even at a more aggressive 5% withdrawal

---

[164] Ibid.

rate, this inflation-adjusted $1,040,000 in 30 years only generates $52,000 in real terms.

Think back to millionaire Bruce Wayne and what it meant to be a millionaire in the 1960s and 1970s. Back then, few middle-class families dared to dream of being millionaires. But today, retiring as a millionaire may only provide for a middle-class lifestyle, and in the future, it may mean even less. As we saw with our calculations above, by annually saving the current 401(k) maximum over a 30-year period, you could become a millionaire—almost a multimillionaire. But while you may be a millionaire, you may barely generate a middle-class income in retirement. That's certainly not enough to live in stately Wayne Manor and afford to keep Alfred the Butler on the payroll!

> *Of course, these are only estimates, as the estimated growth rate of a linear 7% return is unlikely and an inflation rate of 3% is also an estimate. Also, the maximum 401(k) contribution may rise; so this is intended to serve only as an indication of the growth of the current maximum 401(k) plan limit under one unlikely return scenario. Your result could be more or less favorable.*[165]

---

[165] *Savings withdrawal calculator.* (n.d.). Bankrate. Retrieved from http://www.bankrate.com/calculators/savings/savings-withdrawal-calculator-tool.aspx (accessed 17 January 2016).

The Taxation of Defined Contribution 401(k) Plans and Social Security

It's easy to see that taxes are a big drag on middle-class, affluent, and high-income workers, but many people don't realize that even during retirement, income from social security may be taxed, and income from pensions and 401(k) withdrawals are taxed as ordinary income. In 2016, the 25% tax bracket starts at $75,301 for married couples filing jointly,[166] so pension income and 401(k) withdrawals over this amount are going to be taxed at 25%—and this doesn't even include state income taxes, which in some states can total up to 10% or higher.[167]

While not often discussed, one of the most significant drawbacks with saving inside a 401(k) plan is that every dollar is subject to ordinary income taxes upon withdrawal.[168] The same is true for a pre-tax IRA, where any pre-tax contributions and all earnings are taxed at the time of withdrawal. These IRA withdrawals are taxed as ordinary income and the tax rate is based on your income in the year of the withdrawal.[169] My experience tells me many people do not know this, and those who will be fortunate enough to retire with some other sources of income are often surprised to see the severe impact that 401(k) withdrawals can have on their tax return. For those in the

---

[166] *Taxes and tax brackets*. (n.d.). Bankrate. Retrieved from http://www.bankrate.com/finance/taxes/tax-brackets.aspx (accessed 17 June 2016).

[167] *States with the highest and lowest taxes*. (n.d.). Turbo Tax. Retrieved from https://turbotax.intuit.com/tax-tools/tax-tips/Taxes-101/States-with-the-Highest-and-Lowest-Taxes/INF23232.html (accessed 17 June 2016).

[168] Light, Larry. (26 July 2015). *401(k) or Roth IRA: Which is best?* Forbes. Retrieved from http://www.forbes.com/sites/lawrencelight/2015/07/26/401k-or-roth-ira-which-is-best/

[169] *How are IRA withdrawals taxed?* (n.d.). Investopedia. Retrieved from http://www.investopedia.com/ask/answers/102714/how-are-ira-withdrawals-taxed.asp#ixzz3i0dg0Gps (accessed 17 June 2016).

lowest tax brackets, this is less of an issue, but for middle-class and affluent retirees, the impact can be significant.

The next time you take a look at your 401(k) statement, it is important to understand that *it's not all your money*. The government will tax all 401(k) withdrawals as ordinary income—even your gains. And this is true during life or after death. Astute students of the tax code may note that this may seem a little punitive in that investment gains made outside of qualified retirement plans such as a 401(k) plans may be taxed at more favorable dividend or capital gains rates. Dividend and capital gains tax rates currently max out at only 20% for qualified investments[170] (plus some potential taxes from the Pension Protection and Affordable Care Act). This means the taxation of 401(k) plan withdrawals will be, for most Americans, *at their most punitive federal tax rate*. And if there is a year where you need to make sizable withdrawals from your 401(k) plan (e.g., for a wedding, a new roof, etc.), you could actually push yourself into a higher tax bracket. This underscores the need to manage your sources of cash flow in retirement so you can manage your tax bill and keep more of your money!

Also keep in mind that your social security income may also be taxed. If half of your social security benefit + your adjusted gross income + any nontaxable interest you earn exceeds $25,000 for a single filer (or $32,000 for a couple), you may owe taxes on as much as 50% of your social security benefits. A higher tax rate may result if these same income sources are over $34,000 for a single filer (or $44,000 for couples). Above these thresholds, you may need to pay income

---

[170] *Dividends and other distributions.* (n.d.). IRS. Retrieved from http://www.irs.gov/publications/p17/ch08.html (accessed 17 June 2016).

tax on 85% of your social security payments.[171] Approximately 40% of social security beneficiaries have to pay taxes on their benefits.[172]

Roth Provisions Inside 401(k) Plans and Roth IRAs

One way of getting around this tax hit in your retirement is to utilize a Roth provision inside a 401(k) plan, or if you are eligible, a Roth IRA. Keep in mind, however, when you participate in a Roth 401(k), you trade off the loss of a tax deduction now, for tax-free withdrawals later. However, many people, especially higher earners, don't want to miss out on the current tax deduction, so they often prefer to contribute to a 401(k) plan. This is a difficult and complex decision, but generally speaking, if you are going to retire soon and into a much lower tax bracket, then a traditional 401(k) contribution that gives you a tax deduction now might make sense. Alternatively, if you are young and in a lower tax bracket now than you expect to be in later, a Roth contribution may make eminent sense. The approach will be similar if no employer-sponsored plan is available, and you are considering your own tax-deductible IRA or a Roth IRA using after-tax dollars. In many cases, opting for the Roth option can serve a younger investor better.

Subject to just a few rules, the Roth provision inside a 401(k) plan and the Roth IRA each allow for tax-free growth that can later be withdrawn tax-free. Furthermore, younger workers typically are not in their peak earning years, so their current tax rate may be lower than it will be later in life when they are earning higher amounts

---

[171] Brandon, Emily. (9 February 2015). *How to reduce taxes on your social security payments*. U.S. News & World Report. Retrieved from http://money.usnews.com/money/retirement/articles/2015/02/09/how-to-reduce-taxes-on-your-social-security-payments

[172] Ibid.

of money. Therefore, the current tax benefits offered by a pre-tax contribution into a 401(k) plan do not benefit them all that much; however, a Roth provision allows the contribution and all that growth to be withdrawn in retirement with no tax. The Roth 401(k) and Roth IRA are often underutilized due to the current tax deduction of a traditional 401(k) or IRA being so hard to pass up. The tax-free withdrawals of a Roth are subject to IRS restrictions, so review them carefully or consult your tax advisor before making withdrawals.

One of the most difficult situations occurs when young, high earners have little or no net worth but are still in high tax brackets. This is because we have an income tax system that taxes income, even though the objective is to tax the wealthy. Remember, earning a high income and being wealthy do not necessarily equate. For instance, young physicians and attorneys in their late 20s, and even well into their 30s or early 40s, can find themselves in a situation where they are high earners, but may still have a low net worth due to student loan debt. After paying income tax and making student loan payments, they may struggle to find discretionary income for saving. Then, once they do save, they are hit with taxes on their taxable investment income.

> Young physicians and attorneys in their late 20s, and even well into their 30s or early 40s, can find themselves in a situation where they are high earners, but may still have a low net worth due to student loan debt.

Taxes on investments create a significant headwind for young investors, and require them to save even more if they want to build a net worth that allows them to be rewarded for all their studying and hard work. For these young, high earners, it is a very tough decision to invest in a Roth 401(k) because they give up the immediate tax benefit of a more traditional 401(k) plan. That is why I often suggest participating in a traditional 401(k) and using other complementary strategies that are tax efficient in retirement.[173]

But like all aspects of financial planning, everyone's situation is different. Each person must carefully consider the impacts of his or her decisions from a comprehensive standpoint; all these decisions should be made in conjunction with your tax advisor and with an understanding of your overall financial plan.

How Can You Improve Your 401(k)?

The biggest thing anyone can do to get the most out of a 401(k) is to maximize the allowable contribution. Fund it as much as you can! And, if you are relatively young, consider using the Roth provision. If your plan doesn't allow for Roth contributions, then talk to your plan administrator about adding one.

If you are unable to "max out" your contributions, then a good strategy might be to add automatic increases to the salary percentage you are able to defer into your plan. Your plan administrator can easily handle this for you. Many plans allow for annual, automatic increases as a way to help people make a commitment to their retirement planning.

The financial industry is aware of the severe underfunding inside retirement plans, as is the government. There have been new developments in recent years, such as allowing companies to automatically enroll new hires into their 401(k) plans (automatic enrollment) and allowing automatic increases to take place. It is smart to take advantage of any tool that helps you get to your goals quicker.

---

[173] Avallone, Mark. (2 August 2015). *High income, high tax, and low savings: 3 financial tips to help break the Gen X poverty triangle*. Forbes. Retrieved from http://www.forbes.com/sites/markavallone/2015/08/02/high-income-high-tax-and-low-savings-3-financial-tips-to-help-break-the-gen-x-poverty-triangle/

The Biggest 401(k) Trap to Avoid

One of the biggest traps inside any 401(k) plan may be the ability to borrow money. Borrowing from a retirement plan is one of the biggest mistakes an individual can make. When a non-retiree, who is not experiencing a major life tragedy, asks me about a loan from a retirement plan, I always ask, "If you need money so desperately now, what are you going to do when you no longer want to work or are able to work? Why are you borrowing now when you are young and healthy, and taking from funds that you will need later in life when you will be more vulnerable?" These questions are, of course, rhetorical and intended to demonstrate how serious the retirement challenge is and why borrowing against your retirement savings is usually a big mistake.

Unfortunately, short-term thinking satisfies the immediate concerns and often wins out. But regulations allow for loans from retirement plans, and plan sponsors usually allow them as well. If it were up to me, I would eliminate—or at least severely reduce—an individual's ability to borrow from a 401(k) plan. After all, people didn't borrow from their pension plans during the decades when pensions were prominent. And look at how much those plans are revered. Borrowing from a 401(k) plan is one of the cardinal sins that every investor should avoid. Not only are you robbing from your hard-earned savings, you usually have to pay fees and interest on the loan amount to boot. You may also be subjecting yourself to an immediate and aggressive repayment schedule. Most loans are required to be paid back in five years, and if they aren't, they can be considered a taxable distribution.

As I said earlier, the rules and provisions around 401(k) plans are far from ideal, and being able to borrow from your retirement savings is just about one of the worst financial decisions you can possibly make.

Summary

For all its flaws, a 401(k) plan still offers one of the best ways to save on an automatic, pre-tax basis before the money hits your checking account.

- Start early, maximize any company 401(k) match, have a sound investment strategy, and don't cash out when changing jobs.[174]

- Try to maximize your contributions, but if you cannot, try deferring 1% more of your salary every year until you get to the maximum allowed salary deferral amount. Increasing your contributions at the same time you receive a raise may be an effective way to raise your retirement contributions and not feel like your take home pay is taking too much of a hit.

- Be sure to defer in every pay period because many employers match to each paycheck's salary deferral, not a total amount based on your annual contribution. By contributing in every pay period, you will benefit from the matching employer contributions in every pay period. At the start of the year, target a deferral amount that you need to make each pay period through the end of the year in order to get the full match. Your 401(k) plan administrator should be willing to help you with this calculation.

- Be mindful that during any job change there may be a period of ineligibility before you can participate in your new company's 401(k) plan. If that is the case, please try to save into a personal brokerage or bank account during that time

---

[174] *Five habits of 401(k) millionaires: They start early, maximize the company match, and have a sound investment strategy.* (1 January 2014). Fidelity Viewpoints, Fideltiy. Retrieved from https://www.fidelity.com/viewpoints/tcm:526-124671-9451.comp

period. Not having a regular automatic savings plan can have deleterious effects on your long-term planning.

- Younger workers, as well as others in certain situations, should consider utilizing the Roth provision that may be available in their 401(k) plan.

- Young, high earners have a tough decision as to whether the tax deduction now or the tax-free income later is better for them. A combination of the "tax deduction now" and "tax-efficient strategies for later" is oftentimes a good strategy.

- If you are not eligible for a qualified retirement plan through your employer, then max out either a personal Individual Retirement Account (IRA) or a Roth IRA.

- Even if you reach the IRS limits and max out your contributions, you will likely need to save in other accounts, as well. Fund your retirement according to your personal needs—not based on a limit set by the IRS.

- If you have or are eligible to receive a pension, you are among the fortunate. Determine if your estimated pension amount will be enough for you to reach all your goals. If it isn't, start saving to fund the expected shortfall.

- If you don't have a pension, and you are in your 40s and haven't started saving, consider getting a job that has pension benefits. If you know you are unwilling or unable to save, a pension might be your best option. While there is no guarantee that the pension plan will continue, at least you are giving yourself a better chance of avoiding a major downsizing of your lifestyle later in life.

- Integrate the implications of taxes in all your investment and saving decisions. Understand that all your distributions from your 401(k) plan are subject to income taxes and that much of your social security income may also be taxable. For all tax-related matters, consult a tax professional.

- Avoid borrowing from your 401(k) or any retirement plan. Only consider loans for the most serious of circumstances, and even then carefully reconsider. Borrowing from a retirement plan is a huge mistake on many levels.

- Remember, there is no retirement income fairy. I wish it were that easy!

CHAPTER 9

Countdown to Financial Freedom

Every decade of your life holds both opportunities and challenges around earning, saving, and building a plan that can help secure your financial stability. Financial planning is a continuum and a lifelong process. The principles I offer for those in their 20s and 30s are often still relevant even if you are in your 50s. If you've failed to plan at an early age or have been impacted by any of the three Ds—disability, divorce, or death of a partner—financial success may seem farther away, but it is not impossible to reach. Remember Patti Morton from chapter 1? Like many men and women in their 50s and 60s, she found a career later in life that allowed her to recoup financially from losses and lack of planning.

I've developed the guide below as a quick resource to help you identify financial steps you can take advantage of at every decade of your life, from your 20s through your 60s.

In Your 20s

You are fortunate to be young. Take advantage of it by following these tips and strategies as soon as possible.

❱ **Pick your path.** There is no one-size-fits-all path to success. If you've gone straight to work out of high school, or if you have been hustling a few jobs while still in school, you might be happy to have a steady paycheck, and you might be financially ahead of your college graduate peers. A college degree is not something I consider essential for financial success. There are many millionaires who never went to college—and not all of them started a tech firm. Many are blue-collar millionaires who started in landscaping, real estate, sales, and construction, or in a valuable trade, becoming licensed electricians, master plumbers, or experts in other crafts. These skills allowed them to start companies and earn success on their own terms. So if college and graduate degrees are not for you, don't let your determination waiver. If you do, however, have a professional or graduate degree, or simply a college degree in a career-based major that you are passionate about, that can still be a very solid start to reaching your financial goals. No matter which path you chose, being passionate, focused, and determined will get you a long way.

❱ **Focus on your earning power.** Other than gifts or an inheritance, the money you accumulate during life will be from your earnings. A primary focus in your 20s should be developing a set of skills that are useful in the marketplace. The demand for your skills can set the stage for career advancement, increased job satisfaction, and greater income.[175] In turn, your higher earnings can lead to more discretionary

---

[175] Rapacon, Stacy. (January 2015) *10 financial commandments for your 20s.* Kiplinger. Retrieved from http://www.kiplinger.com/article/saving/T063-C006-S001-10-financial-commandments-for-your-20s.html

income that can be used to fund long-term financial goals. Before you can manage your money, you have to earn some!

- **Build liquidity.** Once you start earning, it's important to build some liquidity. Liquidity is money that, while saved, is available to you for emergencies, important purchases, or a down payment on a home. You can't build liquidity if you are spending all of your take-home pay. Get in the habit of living on less than your total paycheck, and automatically save the surplus.

- **Wield the power of compounding interest**. The earlier you start to save, the more time you give your money to grow. When your money grows, you earn interest on both your initial investment amount and on the interest it has already earned. That is "compounding interest." No one stays young forever, so start compounding that interest now for more benefit.

- **Beat the temptation to spend**. As a 20-something, you may be able to finally afford some of the things you've been dreaming about: maybe a cool apartment in the city, a nice car, the latest technology products, or dining out and going to clubs. Perhaps the biggest optional expense that young people incur is funding their entertainment and social life. Sure it's more fun than planning for your financial future; but starting a savings plan now while you're young is one of the best financial moves you can make, and can put you far ahead of your peers down the road. Before you spend, consider what you want more: material things and fun today or the freedom of not needing to work at some point in your life when you're still young enough to enjoy it.

- **Consider carefully before deciding to rent or buy.** A lot of young people today rent apartments in major urban areas and put off home buying and even car buying. This can save money on things like house repairs, property taxes, utility bills, extra furniture, and car ownership, maintenance, and repair. This renting trend was spurred by the 2008 crash in housing prices, which made younger people skeptical of the financial benefits of home ownership. Many saw what excessive borrowing from home equity can do to a financial plan, and they also learned that home prices do not always rise. These are good lessons to keep in mind. However, it is also important to remember that, at least until excessive borrowing against home equity came along, home mortgage payments provided a form of forced savings and created lasting wealth for many.

- **Remember that cars are a depreciating asset.** Cars almost always depreciate over time, and they can be expensive. The purchase cost, sales tax, registration fees, insurance, repairs, and gas (not to mention speed camera and stoplight tickets), will eat a lot of your budget. If you need to own a car, buy below your budget to help keep overall cost of car ownership down. And if you only occasionally need transportation, forego buying and look to the sharing economy as a way to save. Services like Zipcar, Uber, and Lyft are changing the landscape and may help you avoid the expense and hassle of owning a car. Later in life, when you have excess cash flow, you can consider splurging on a car of your dreams, but for now, avoid this spending trap if you can.

- **Educate yourself about personal finance.** Start reading articles and books on personal financial planning. Be deliberate and don't depend solely on any one piece of advice. Read several sources to see what works best for you and your goals. If reading isn't your thing, take some classes at a local community college or find a Certified Financial Planner™ you would like to work with, and hire him or her to help guide you.

- **Get a written financial plan for yourself or for you and your family.** One of the best things you can do for your financial future is to complete a written financial plan. Looking at a plan with the actual numbers in black and white can have a tremendous impact on your progress. Much like the commitment you get from having a personal trainer versus going to the gym on your own, if you engage a financial planner you might add another level of commitment to your planning.

- **Protect your biggest "asset:" your income.** Think of your *future earning power* as your biggest asset. Consider protecting it with disability income insurance. The younger you are, the less expensive disability insurance will be. With Millennials and even older workers increasingly changing jobs, you may have gaps in coverage or be stuck with an inferior group policy. Consider getting a personal disability policy that is portable, so you can carry it with you wherever you live or work.

- **Start a retirement savings plan.** Once you have an adequate amount of cash liquidity, begin to save for longer-term goals. Saving on a tax-efficient basis may make sense. If you work at a company that offers a matching contribution on a 401(k) plan or other qualified retirement plan, you may want to consider maxing out whatever matching benefit is available. Whether you're using the immediate tax benefits of a traditional 401(k) plan or the future tax benefits of a Roth IRA, it's important that you take advantage of these tax shelters as early in life as possible. One of the best aspects of these plans is that you can fund your 401(k) through automatic payroll deductions; and you can fund a Roth IRA with automatic transfers from your checking account the day after your paycheck is deposited. Start educating yourself or consult with your tax advisor or investment professional on which plan is best for you.

- **Don't let job changes slow down the growth in your retirement assets.** In the new economy, younger people are changing jobs more frequently. At your new company, there may be a waiting period up to 18 months before you're eligible for the 401(k) plan. If you are subject to a waiting period, consider setting up your own automatic investment until your 401(k) plan eligibility kicks in. You can direct your savings into either a Roth IRA or a traditional IRA if you are eligible, or any savings or investment account. Just be sure to consider any such accounts as long-term investments and keep them out of easy reach!

- **Roth provisions in your 401(k) plan or a Roth IRA can be very attractive.** While you are in a low, marginal tax bracket, the current tax deduction in a traditional 401(k) or IRA is not as attractive as when you are in a higher tax bracket. Consider the benefits of a Roth contribution into your 401(k) or a Roth IRA.

- **Reduce or pay off any student debt.** The class of 2015 was the most indebted in American history (as of May 2015) with the average graduate owing more than $35,000.[176] This hefty sum becomes more problematic because it is subject to significant interest rates, typically in the mid-single digits depending on the type of borrowing plan.[177] These rates may be lower than historical student loan interest rates; nonetheless, they can bury even disciplined borrowers in interest payments. Choosing to accelerate student loan repayment can bypass much of this problem. It will require that you select a student loan repayment option with a shorter timeframe. Of the repayment plans currently offered by the federal government, most have either a 10-year or 25-year window.[178] Assuming a 6.84% interest rate on an average $35,000 note, the difference between these timeframes becomes critical: a 10-year borrower will pay $13,400 in interest while the 25-year borrower will pay $38,100, which is greater than the size of the original loan!

- **Educate yourself.** A three-year survey of 43,000 college students found that only 58% feel prepared to manage their

---

[176] Sparshott, Jeffrey. (8 May 2015). *Congratulations, class of 2015: You're the most indebted ever (for now)*. The Wall Street Journal. Retrieved from http://blogs.wsj.com/economics/2015/05/08/congratulations-class-of-2015-youre-the-most-indebted-ever-for-now/

[177] *What are Average Student Loan Rates?* (13 June 2015). Credible Labs. Retrieved from https://www.credible.com/blog/student-lending/what-are-average-student-loan-interest-rates/

[178] *Understanding repayment: Repayment plans.* (n.d.). Federal Student Aid, an Office of the U.S. Department of Education. Retrieved from https://studentaid.ed.gov/sa/repay-loans/understand/plans

money.[179] The survey also found, however, that those students who had received a formal education in financial management were significantly more likely to be financially responsible than their peers.[180] Even if formal education is not available to you, teaching yourself about personal budgeting and finance is an excellent idea. With the explosion of information on the Internet, knowledge is only a few clicks away.

- **Build your credit score.** Typically, the younger you are, the lower your credit score.[181] But this doesn't have to be the case for you. If you can proactively build your creditworthiness at a young age, you can receive better loan terms for the rest of your life. Some of the most important tips for boosting your score are (1) closely monitor your credit score and reports for errors and fraud, (2) build an emergency fund so that you never miss bills because of unexpected expenses, and (3) set up automatic withdrawals to pay your bills consistently and on time.[182]

---

[179] *The Financial Brand.* (29 July 2015). Higher One. Retrieved from http://www.higherone.com/press/414-the-financial-brand

[180] Malcolm, Hadley. (8 April 2014). *Financial literacy education has lasting impact.* USA Today. Retrieved from http://www.usatoday.com/story/money/personalfinance/2014/04/08/financial-literacy-college-students/7296185/

[181] *What is the average credit score in America by age and state?* (n.d.). Credit Card Forum. Retrieved from http://creditcardforum.com/blog/what-is-the-average-credit-score/ (22 June 2016).

[182] Lee, Jenna. (26 March 2015). *5 smart credit habits to start in your 20s.* U.S. News & World Report. Retrieved from http://money.usnews.com/money/blogs/my-money/2015/03/26/5-smart-credit-habits-to-start-in-your-20s

In Your 30s

These years can be the beginning of an accelerated earnings trajectory so plan wisely for how you will build a sound financial foundation.

- **Live beneath your means.** Determine your monthly cash outflow amounts. Set up a cash-flow worksheet and a guideline limit for discretionary expenses. If you're a parent or single head of household, saving money can be a bit more difficult, but providing a solid future for your child or children can be a great motivator. If you're partnered and sharing expenses, the benefits of a double income may help you create extra income to save—if you choose to live below your means. However, households can be tempted to overspend as they build their life together and accumulate "stuff." This is a good time to let your written financial plan help you avoid excessive spending.

- **Think strategically about your career planning.** Finding the right balance between professional time and personal or family time while trying to maximize earnings can be tricky. You may face decisions about your career that have implications for the amount of time or quality of time you'll spend with family. Your decisions may also impact your family's financial balance. Think strategically as you build your career in order to strike whatever balance you and your family need. In my work as a financial advisor, I've seen how financial struggles can be a strain on couples. It's helpful to communicate clearly about money, balance your priorities, and get a mutually agreed upon plan in place. If talking about money is a difficult dynamic in your household, find a professional who can be an independent voice

- **Become an owner.** Young people often have an entrepreneurial spirit and see the benefits of being an owner, but starting a company has its challenges. A popular alternative among young people is to join an entrepreneurial company and gain access to ownership without assuming the risk of their own start-up. Joining a forward-thinking company with a generous stock option plan can eventually be a lucrative source of wealth should your employer experience success. Look into equity ownership options at your company or any company you may be considering joining.

  I am not just talking about small start-ups that attract a lot of young talent. There are plenty of Fortune 500 companies that have stock-grant and other bonus programs as part of their compensation packages. I have worked with many people who were granted seemingly modest stock options and grant programs as part of their compensation. Over time, as their company stock performed well, so did the value of their shares. If you are fortunate to land with the right company, you may be able to accumulate a fair amount of wealth this way.

- **If you have children, consider setting up a college savings plan for them now.** The average age at which a mother has her first child is 25.6 years.[183] For women with college degrees, that number skews slightly older. In either situation, this

---

[183] *The World Fact Book*. (n.d.). Library, CIA. Retrieved from https://www.cia.gov/library/publications/the-world-factbook/fields/2256.html (accessed 28 June 2016)

means that many people in their 30s either already have or soon will have their own little bundles of joy. But with the joy of becoming a parent, comes additional expense and burden of paying for higher education. As I have discussed, four-year colleges have become an astronomical expense for parents. Making use of tax-advantaged savings instruments at a young age is a good way to address this expense.

- **Pay off non-mortgage debt.** Carrying high-cost, nontax-deductible debt is one of the worst mistakes anyone serious about wealth accumulation can make. Sometimes a young person winds up with debt from decisions made when they were a teenager. Student loans and any other nontax-deductible debt should be eradicated as quickly as possible (unless it carries a very low interest rate, which is usually not the case).

- **Benefit from low, tax-deductible, mortgage interest rates.** Renting allows flexibility and can carry a lower total monthly cost versus owning a home. Alternatively, low interest rates can make home ownership attractive. Furthermore, the interest you pay on a mortgage is one of the few remaining tax deductions for individuals (and married couples). Being able to deduct interest on mortgage debt lowers the cost of your home ownership, and with each amortizing mortgage payment, you reduce your outstanding principal balance. If you avoid the temptation to borrow against home equity, eventually you may build equity in your home. Home equity is the amount of your home's value less its debt.

Keep in mind, however, that even though rates are low, there is still an after-tax interest cost to any mortgage. Some people strongly prefer to have little or no debt at all. If that is the case for you, look to a shorter amortization schedule such as a 15-year loan, which often offers a lower rate and a lower amount of interest cost over the life of the mortgage versus a 30-year structure (albeit at the cost of a higher monthly payment as you are paying more principal down each month). The long-term historical returns of the U.S. stock market (roughly averaging 10% during the 20th century) have been greater than the recent cost of a 30-year mortgage (under 4%).[184,185] Therefore, I am not averse to utilizing prudent leverage when buying a home and hopefully building up home equity.

> **Consider a convertible term life insurance policy.** The average age for a first marriage in the United States is 27 for women and 29 for men.[186] This means a significant portion of 30-somethings are presently in some sort of committed relationship. This also may mean that someone in your life is relying on you to provide financial stability. If you have children, you also have very important financial obligations. Therefore, purchasing and maintaining relatively inexpensive term life insurance policies for both spouses—regardless of employment status—may be beneficial for your family's financial freedom. As discussed

---

[184] DeGrace, Tom. (30 July 2014). *The historical rate of return for the stock market since 1900.* Stock Pick System, Stock Systems Inc. Retrieved from http://www.stockpickssystem.com/historical-rate-of-return/

[185] *Average 30 year fixed mortgage rates.* (n.d.). Mortgage Daily News. Retrieved from http://www.mortgagenewsdaily.com/data/30-year-mortgage-rates.aspx (accessed 29 June 2016).

[186] Barkhorn, Eleanor. (15 March 2013) *Getting married later is great for college-educated women.* The Atlantic. Retrieved from http://www.theatlantic.com/sexes/archive/2013/03/getting-married-later-is-great-for-college-educated-women/274040/

in chapter 7, the death of a spouse can be devastating for the survivor, and especially for minor children.

When looking at term life insurance, consider a "convertible" term life insurance policy. Term has a lower annual cost than permanent coverage, but it is, as its name implies, a temporary solution. This somewhat temporary nature of term life insurance helps explain why it requires less money to purchase than a similar amount of permanent death benefit product. With a convertible term policy, you gain the ability to convert your term insurance policy into a permanent policy without a medical exam or other underwriting. Also note that term coverage typically increases in price after a set period of time, whereas your permanent policy will likely not have price increases. With your convertible term policy, you can help protect your family and financial plan now and when you are older, even if there is a change in your health. When you convert your term policy (or a portion of it) into a permanent policy, your death benefit is permanent, provided you make your payments. This can help you leave money to your children, spouse, grandchildren, or even parents or other family members who may depend upon you for support. And remember, the later in life you apply for life insurance, the higher the cost and risk that you become uninsurable.

Everyone's situation will vary, and your own considerations will determine how much, if any, life insurance might be prudent. For example, if there is an income disparity between newlyweds, the spouses may want to consider life insurance at the onset of their marriage. Moreover, expectant parents may want to consider applying for life insurance before their baby arrives.

⟫ **Consider the tax advantages of permanent whole life insurance.** Although typically thought of as a way to protect a family from an unexpected event, whole life insurance (also known as permanent life insurance) can also offer certain tax advantages. A permanent policy can allow you to allocate an amount over your premium and receive your cash value later, with potentially favorable income tax implications. If you are a young, high earner, you may be in a position to overfund a policy—input more money than what is needed just for the death benefit. Given the high tax environment we face, and with taxes showing little chance of abating, accumulating cash value inside a life insurance policy may be ideal for a young high earner.

While the primary reason to purchase a life insurance product is usually the death benefit, a young person can significantly overfund the policy relative to the cost of the death benefit, thereby also making it a potential wealth accumulation vehicle. Life insurance products contain fees, such as mortality and expense charges, and may contain restrictions, such as surrender periods; but they also offer valuable, potential tax benefits. Please keep in mind that overfunding too much can turn the life insurance policy into a Modified Endowment Contract (MEC), creating adverse tax consequences. Work closely with your financial advisor and the insurance company to adhere to the limits. When the IRS allows certain benefits, they usually have a lot of rules and guidelines you will need to adhere to; so also consult with a tax professional on any tax-driven strategy.

- **Maintain a sound Investment portfolio that is consistent with your personal objectives and risk tolerance level.** As long as you're working, you should start saving for retirement as early as possible—that's critical given the benefits of compound growth. While the *allocation* of your investments should change over the course of your life, generally the younger you are, the more risk you should consider taking. Younger investors who have more time to ride out bear markets can maintain riskier investments like stocks—this may have a higher probability of higher growth over a long period of time.[187] You may now be seeing the effects of market fluctuation on your investments and learning your emotional tolerance for different levels of risk. Understand your emotions and how they may affect your investments so that you can better invest without letting your emotions take the lead.

- **Consider "maxing the match."** As in your 20s, consider at least maximizing your 401(k) contributions in order meet your company's matching policy (if it has one); in other words "max the match." Be sure to make salary deferrals from your paycheck into your 401(k) plan in every pay period, because many employers match to each pay period's salary deferral; not to your total annual salary. Higher earners should try to reach the maximum IRS contribution limits during the year and maximize any matching employer contributions in every pay period. At the start of the year, target a deferral

---

[187] Geary, Leslie Haggin. (n.d.). *Retirement planning for people in their 30s.* Bankrate. Retrieved from http://www.bankrate.com/finance/financial-literacy/retirement-planning-for-people-in-their-30s-1.aspx (accessed 29 June 2016).

amount that you need to make each pay period through the end of the year in order to get the full match. Your 401(k) plan administrator should be willing to help you with this calculation. And consider utilizing the Roth 401(k) provision if it is available.

- **Review your written financial plan.** I highly recommend regular reviews and updates of your written financial plan. Regular reviews help you focus on how your goals are evolving, whether you are on pace to reach your goals, and what steps are needed to achieve better outcomes if you're behind.

- **Be tax aware.** The tax code constantly changes. Understand how taxes impact you and how you can benefit. If your situation has complexity, work with a trusted, qualified tax professional to help guide your tax planning.

- **Get some estate documents completed and signed.** You've had an estate plan from the minute you were born: it is what your state of residence determines for you based on existing law. And it generally stays in place unless you override it, or parts of it, with your own planning documents. Once you are married or have children, it becomes more important to create basic documents, such as a will, to leave assets to whom you want them to go. Others, such as those who are married, have children, or have sizable assets, may want to explore which types of trusts are beneficial for them. Most importantly, consider naming legal guardians for each of your children, establishing medical directives, and (carefully) naming your power of attorney.

In Your 40s

These are prime earning years, so make the most of them.

> **Continue to maintain cash reserves, but not more than needed.** Unforeseeable events happen, and they can affect anyone at any time. Rather than dipping into your retirement savings to repair that leaky roof or pay for a hospital visit, keep some cash available for unexpected expenses like these.[188] It is also more tax efficient to withdraw from liquid, taxable accounts than from nonqualified retirement plan assets. It is important, however, that you not keep so much money in cash that you're needlessly foregoing investment opportunities. Many people were turned off by stocks during the 2008 crash, and as a result, they missed the subsequent stock market rally by holding too much cash. A proper portfolio balance and taking the emotion out of investing is important for an investor's success.

> **Be mindful of the tax code and utilize it to your advantage.** If your income has risen, and hopefully it has, then your income tax burden has risen too. Consult with your CPA for specific strategies on the benefits and drawbacks of a Traditional 401(k) versus a Roth 401(k). Also consider any tax-favored products for your taxable accounts. Understand the role of cash value inside a whole life insurance policy. Once you are in your 50s, it is harder to make the benefits of a permanent policy work as well as when you are younger. If you have

---

[188] Lerner, Michele. (2 May 2013). *6 financial planning tips for 40-somethings.* Fox Business. Retrieved from http://www.foxbusiness.com/personal-finance/2013/05/02/six-financial-planning-tips-for-40-somethings/

children, and if you have not done so already, consider setting up a college savings plan. Be sure to continue to consult with your tax advisor as tax laws—and opportunities—can change.

> **Continue with your debt reduction strategy.** If you implemented a debt payoff strategy in your 30s, it may have taken you this long to achieve its objectives. If you're still working on reducing and eliminating (non-mortgage) debt, look for ways to accelerate the process when your income grows. Keep in mind, I am not referring to debt on your residence, which may be low cost and offer tax benefits. Student loans (unless eligible for special forgiveness from the government) and consumer debt likely offer no tax benefits and are often higher cost, so they should be avoided or eliminated.

> **Consider not only maxing out your company match, but also reaching the IRS allowed limits.** Hopefully, you haven't waited until your 40s to at least begin meeting your employer's 401(k) match (if available). But during your 40s, you should also aspire to "up your game" by meeting the statutory maximum for 401(k) contribution each year, which is $18,000 in 2016.[189] Again, every time that you don't take full advantage of tax provisions like this one, you're leaving money on the table. Earlier, I noted that even maximum contributions to a 401(k) plan may not be enough savings for your retirement. In review of your written financial plan, which should be updated every one or two years, determine

---

[189] *6 Tips for financial planning in your 40s.* (n.d.). Bankrate. Retrieved from http://www.bankrate.com/finance/savings/financial-planning-in-your-40s-4.aspx (accessed 22 June 2016).

how much more than this maximum 401(k) contribution limit you need to save elsewhere in order to reach your goals.

> **Be disciplined about not borrowing from your 401(K) plan.** In 2013, 2.4% of people raided their 401(k) due to some form of hardship.[190] Treating your 401(k) as an emergency piggy bank has a litany of negative consequences. It typically subjects withdrawn funds to a higher rate of taxation than they would likely be subject to in retirement. You also incur tax penalties for withdrawing 401(k) funds prematurely. Finally, and perhaps worst of all, you prevent the withdrawn funds from contributing to the compounding interest of your account. Borrowing from a 401(k) plan is one of the worst mistakes an individual investor can make.

> **Continue to be a growth-oriented investor.** You are still young enough to ride out the market's ups and downs. Giving in to emotion and worry about losing money in the stock market may not work to your advantage. Life expectancies are lengthening, and you need your money to grow more than the rate of inflation to maintain purchasing power over your lifetime.

> **Go get a pension.** If you haven't started to save, or if you are not the type of person who will start saving, look for a position with a company or a state or local government that offers a pension plan. There are still enough years for you to accumulate a meaningful pension benefit. Keep in mind

---

[190] *Tapping your 401(k) also helps Uncle Sam pay his bills.* (6 May 2014). Bloomberg. Retrieved from http://www.bloomberg.com/infographics/2014-05-05/americans-raid-their-401k-piggy-banks.html

the possibility that pension terms can change, including the terms of your expected payout. But if you haven't started saving and don't think you can, gaining access to a pension might be a smart strategy.

> **Utilize various aspects of your group benefits package.** Be sure to review your health insurance options for the plan that is a good fit for you and your family. Every American is now eligible for health insurance coverage. Consider if it is advantageous for you to choose a health insurance plan with a high deductible. Also consider if you would benefit from a Health Savings Account (HSA) or a Flexible Spending Account (FSA). And, if you are unable to get approved for a personal life insurance or personal disability income policy, check out what your employer can offer you without your needing to go through the underwriting and approval process.

> **Review your beneficiaries and estate documents.** A review and possible revision of your estate documents makes good sense, especially if you have a parent who relies on you, or if you had a life-changing event such as a divorce, remarriage, or more children.

In Your 50s

By this stage, you have, at least in some part, made the retirement bed you are going to sleep in; but there is still some time to improve your situation and fund your longer-term retirement goals. If you are like many parents, you may have focused on your children earlier in life and are now finally focusing on yourself. Emotionally, I understand this, but financially, it may not have been the best course of action. As the saying goes, you can borrow for your children's college but not for your retirement. In any case, there is still time either to catch up or to solidify your plan. If you are serious, you can make a lot of progress.

- **Monitor your progress relative to your written financial plan**. It is not too late to impact your financial future. Work with your financial advisor to check your financial plan and adjust as needed.

- **Hopefully you have already considered maximizing your contributions to your 401(K) or other qualified retirement plan**. At this age, if your income is near its peak, and you are in a high marginal tax bracket, a traditional 401(k) contribution may be more valuable from a tax perspective than a Roth contribution. This is especially true if you think you will retire into a lower tax bracket.

- **Examine your risk tolerance in light of your personal situation**. It is important to know your risk tolerance. You should carefully consider a variety of factors, including whether your household has one or two earners, what kind of job security you have, where you are in your financial plan, and what inheritances you may receive. Consider, too, your life expectancy. If, for example, your family tree has many relatives with longevity and a strong genetic history, you may want to factor in the need for a continued growth focus in your investment portfolio to keep up with inflation over the coming decades, or you may want to focus on building reliable lifetime income sources. If you are employed with a company that is struggling and your continued employment is uncertain, you might want to invest more like a near retiree, with a lower allocation to stocks and a portion in more stable investments.[191] Each person's goals vary, so take careful inventory of your situation, and plan accordingly in advance of your retirement.

> **Begin to shift your investment portfolio into more moderate assets.** As you approach your late 50s, you are no longer decades away from retirement; so the booms and busts of the stock market may be difficult to handle emotionally. Plus, many people in their 50s begin experiencing turbulence in their careers or other life challenges, like health issues. It's prudent to have more money available that is not subject to the wide movements that stock investing presents. Furthermore, there is the possibility of a "lost decade" such as the 2000s, during which the S&P 500 returned a -9.1% for the calendar decade. A near retiree should not have all their assets in risky investments, and certainly not all in one asset class, like common stocks.

> **Consider long-term care insurance.** Non-acute care is not covered under most health care policies (it was initially written into the Affordable Care Act but is not a part of the current law due to the huge potential costs of caring for our aging population). The cost of non-acute care has risen dramatically; so many insurers no longer offer long-term care insurance. For married couples, long-term care insurance can protect the healthy spouse, whose assets are also at risk

---

[191] Pollack, Michael A. (6 October 2013). *How to get your 401(k) ready for retirement*. The Wall Street Journal. Retrieved from http://www.wsj.com/articles/SB10001424127887324576304579073053686155322

of being depleted if the other spouse needs prolonged care. For a single person, coverage can provide dignity and peace of mind knowing that affordable care is a possibility. Unless you can self-fund expensive, unexpected, long-term, non-acute care, you need to consider how to protect yourself from these costs. Understand that you have to be "virtually penniless" before Medicaid will pay for nursing home bills, which can average about $91,000 per year, according to a report by Genworth Financial.[192]

> **Prepare for any estate taxes.** If you are fortunate enough to have a sizable estate, and especially if you live in a state with a punitive estate tax structure, talk with an attorney and plan accordingly. Even in the absence of potential estate tax liability, developing a wealth transfer plan may make sense so that your hard-earned assets wind up where you want them.

> **Begin to estimate how much social security you'll receive.** Consider at what specific age you might make your transition into retirement, and estimate your social security benefit (go to www.ssa.gov to calculate your estimates). If you haven't already gotten serious about retirement, you may need to work into your late 60s or early 70s, and that may become physically difficult. Working longer might increase your social security benefit—because the later you take social security, the greater the potential benefit amount—but that might be small consolation for having to work those extra years.

---

[192] *Genworth 2015 cost of care survey: Home care providers, adult day health care facilities, assisted living facilities and nursing homes.* (20 March 2015). Genworth. Retrieved from http://www.dailyfinance.com/2015/04/09/elder-care-costs-keep-climbing-nursing-home-bill/

As you may know, there are concerns about Social Security solvency. I believe a total collapse is highly unlikely, however, means testing may be part of the government's solution at some point in the future. So, be mindful that your social security benefit could be affected. "Means testing" means, generally, that if the government determines that you are wealthy, or that you will not need this cash flow as much as another person, you might see your social security benefits either reduced or taxed more heavily. This could result in a reduced benefit versus what you might have otherwise considered a rock-solid amount of retirement income. If the government takes this step, it will create a *de facto* penalty for those who have worked hard and saved. Unfortunately, we don't know what steps will be taken.

> **if you have not started saving for retirement, there are things you can do, but you must start now.** Start saving immediately, cut back on expenses, and expect to work longer, holding off retirement for later. Many retirees move to lower-cost locales to help stretch their retirement dollars, and this can also be helpful for pre-retirees who started saving late. There are always options. Talking with a financial professional can help you better identify and understand your choices and their impacts.

In Your 60s

You may be comfortable with your finances, but if not, there is still time to improve your financial life. It is also a chance to outline how you will be able to afford your life goals and spend these later years with meaning and vigor.

- **Forecast your retirement cash flow.** While budgets and cash flow worksheets may seem like exercises for young people just getting started, they will be important throughout your financial life. It's imperative that near retirees clearly understand how much they may need to spend on an annual basis.[193] Despite popular myths, your budget after retirement is likely to be somewhat similar to your budget during working years. Therefore, before you make the transition to part-time income or retirement, check to make sure your current savings will be sufficient to generate replacement income.

- **Take corrective actions.** If your retirement income projections are coming up short, now is the time to circle the wagons. If you've been living above your means, do what you can now to start living below your means. If needed, downsize and simplify. Likewise, if your children have moved out of the house, that can be a catalyst for simplifying your lifestyle. If your anticipated shortfall is significant, now is the time to reduce spending on non-essentials, such as clothing, jewelry, electronics, or other toys—tell yourself there's a new sheriff in town, and he doesn't allow self-sabotage any more. Lightening the load that these burdens have placed on your financial picture will give you a new lease on life.

- **Consolidate your retirement accounts.** On average, individuals born between 1957 and 1964 have had 11.7 jobs

---

[193] *Financial planning in your 60s.* (June 2014). Consumer Reports. Retrieved from http://www.consumerreports.org/cro/2014/06/financial-planning-in-your-60s/index.htm

over their working years.[194] This may mean that you have a half-dozen retirement accounts, or even more. Juggling all of those accounts can be difficult, and it can compromise your ability to make sure they're all properly allocated and looked after. Also, having fewer plans may result in a reduction in unnecessary administrative fees that plans often charge (and it might make for less red tape for your heirs should you die earlier than expected). As you age, it becomes more prudent to simplify things, if you haven't taken this step earlier.

> **Plan for inevitable medical expenses.** The number-one cause of personal bankruptcies in the United States is medical expenses.[195] As you age, your annual medical expenses will almost certainly increase. You will become eligible for Medicare benefits at age 65, and these will cover many expenses, but they don't cover everything. Consider purchasing Medicare Supplement Insurance, also known as Medigap. It covers many expenses such as copayments and deductibles that Medicare might otherwise not cover.[196] As of 2010, only 14% of Medicare beneficiaries relied solely on Medicare, which means 86% of beneficiaries recognized the

---

[194] *Number of jobs held, labor market activity, and earnings growth among the youngest baby boomers: Results from a longitudinal survey.* (31 March 2015). News Release (USDL-15-0528). Bureau of Labor Statistics, U.S. Department of Labor. Retrieved from http://www.bls.gov/news.release/pdf/nlsoy.pdf

[195] LaMontagne, Christina. (19 June 2013). *NerdWallet Health finds medical bankruptcy accounts for majority of personal bankruptcies.* NerdWallet. Retrieved from https://www.nerdwallet.com/blog/health/managing-medical-bills/nerdwallet-health-study-estimates-56-million-americans-65-struggle-medical-bills-2013/

[196] *What's Medicare supplement insurance (Medigap)?* (n.d.). Medicare.gov, Centers for Medicare & Medicaid Services. Retrieved from https://www.medicare.gov/supplement-other-insurance/medigap/whats-medigap.html (accessed 29 June 2016).

need to supplement the program with alternative sources of coverage.[197]

> **Visualize how and when your heirs will receive your wealth.** While you're still alive, you have the ability to control to whom, how, and when your hard-earned wealth will be distributed after your death. If you want your financial assets to be passed on in a manner consistent with your objectives and belief system, now is the time to set that up. A trust can help you manage when children and others receive their checks. You can also begin considering if gifts are something you can afford to do. Remember, the federal government has rules around gifting, so be sure to do this in conjunction with your tax and financial advisors. If you are fortunate to have enough assets to create an estate tax issue, advance planning might help reduce that tax liability.

> **Consider various options for gaining lifetime income in retirement.** There are approaches offered by insurance companies that will help manage some of the uncertainty associated with retirement income planning. Carefully look into how some of these may be a good fit for your situation, or consult with your advisor.

> **If your income is insufficient, explore getting a "hobby job" that will generate some added cash flow.** Combining something you enjoy doing with earning extra income is an excellent way to improve your cash flow while having a good time.

---

[197] *Medigap reform: Setting the context for understanding recent proposals.* (13 January 2014). The Henry J. Kaiser Family Foundation. http://kff.org/medicare/issue-brief/medigap-reform-setting-the-context/

- **Manage your tax bill. Ordinary income, capital gains, and dividends all have different tax treatments.** Before you raise cash or sell an asset, consider the tax implications. Especially in years where you need more cash flow than others. Be mindful of the tax implications of any withdrawals and how one-time withdrawals from your 401(k) might raise your marginal tax bracket. Also be aware that investments with high capital gains get a "step-up in cost basis" upon death of the owner so it may make sense to sell these assets only if absolutely needed. By not selling during your lifetime, you may be able to avoid the tax hit on your capital gain.

- **Build a plan consistent with your life goals.** After all your hard work and planning, now is the time to relax and enjoy this phase of life. If you cannot, then work with a financial advisor you know and trust. Meet with them on a regular basis. Let them help you take your plan to a place you feel comfortable and happy with.

Summary

As you can see, financial strategies vary with the changing needs of investors in each decade of their earnings years. If you're serious about planning for your retirement years, familiarize yourself with the differences in the recommended strategies for each decade. Then assess your financial picture to determine which of the strategies might help you and check again periodically for any tactics you might have missed. You and your financial planner and tax professional can fine-tune your specific tactics and objectives to take advantage of current economic conditions—and you can better plan for the future you want.

CHAPTER 10

What's Next?

The amazing thing about your money, finances, and retirement plan is that it's totally up to you whether they become your friends or your adversaries. If you learn to take control of your money, understand your financial situation, and become disciplined enough to stick to your spending and savings plans, then you'll enjoy a favorable and comfortable relationship with your money. If you've read chapter 9, then you know your relationship with money will change over the years as you create a plan, save, learn to discipline yourself, and grow your financial skills.

Follow your plan and, by the time you hit retirement age, you'll be great friends with your money. You will most likely be comfortable with your spending and savings plan and, hopefully, you'll have weathered your life and the challenges it presented. However, if you're starting to save later in life, don't worry. Many people "wake up" late in life or come into a career that finally allows them to save. You may have to be more creative and focused about it at age 40, 50, or 60 than someone who started in their 20s or 30s; but it can be done.

What I have found that helps families and individuals more than anything else is to have honest conversations about their finances. Ask yourself if your current career path and earning capacity can provide for the life you want. If the answer is no, consider broadening your skill set to pursue other career options. If you don't understand finances, learn. Take some classes or read as much as you can about topics that confuse you. If you still want more insight and guidance, find a good financial advisor. A smart way to start that process is to look for a Certified Financial Planner™.

Be mindful not to assign "money matters" solely to one spouse or life partner. Both you and your spouse (if relevant) should be fully involved in making your financial decisions. If the financial brains, so to speak, of the family were to die first, and you were left on your own to figure out the finances, it could be extremely difficult for you at a time when things are already stressful. Likewise, should a divorce come your way, it's difficult to start learning about the funds you have available (which might be a different amount than you thought) and the amount of money you're going to need. Never hand total control of your finances to a partner. Instead, work together toward your retirement and your education about spending and saving. Financial literacy and a better understanding of the challenges that face you and your future are essential to creating the financial freedom you'll want in retirement.

If you've read this far, you know there is little chance of middle-class welfare from the federal or state government in retirement. No government agency is going to swoop in and provide you with extra money so you can take a couple of vacations a year or upgrade your kitchen. It's also unlikely that a rich stranger will leave you a multimillion-dollar inheritance or that you will score big in Vegas. You probably will need to fund your lifestyle from money you have saved, or you will need to continue your employment despite how old you may be. The choice is yours. Your choices now will determine how you get there.

Have a Written Financial Plan

As I have said throughout this book, having a written financial plan in place can be the single most important step you take to evaluate and plan for your financial future. You can even start with a plan you draft at home. Then take that to a qualified planner to flesh it out, explore details, and ask any questions. Your plan doesn't have to be mind-numbingly complex. You don't need to use financial speak, and please don't get intimidated by the process. If you break it down and take it in small bites, it might be easier to handle. You might even find it to be fun and personally satisfying.

Have a Good Savings and Spending Plan and Stick to It

Current indicators show that millions of Americans have inadequate savings and are unable to stop working, despite their age. A recent Gallup poll shows two-thirds of adult Americans are estimated to have no written financial plan.[198] According to a new survey on retirement readiness by Schwab Retirement Plan Services, 35% of the people they surveyed said they were not saving or were not increasing their savings because they didn't want it to affect their current quality of life.[199] In addition, many haven't planned, not because they're irresponsible, but because they're confused about what exactly they need to do.

---

[198] Jacobe, Dennis. (3 June 2013). *One in three Americans prepare detailed household budget.* Gallop. Retrieved from http://www.gallup.com/poll/162872/one-three-americans-prepare-detailed-household-budget.aspx

[199] *Schwab survey finds people prioritize wealth over health, but retirement savings hurdles remain.* (26 August 2015). News Release, Charles Schwab. Retrieved from http://www.aboutschwab.com/images/uploads/inline/8.25.15_2015_Schwab_401_k_Participant_Survey_Release_Final.pdf

There is an education gap, as well. Nearly half of the people surveyed (47%) said the information they received on their 401(k) investment options was more confusing than the materials that explained their health benefits, and we all know what those are like: challenging to say the least! A better understanding of both the role of 401(k) plans and the retirement planning process will be an important challenge for many people.

As a financial advisor, I find it interesting that 67% of the people Schwab interviewed said they thought professional guidance might help them create a plan. More than half said they would like advice on choosing 401(k) investments, and 49% said they believed they would see improved investment performance if they sought professional help. It makes sense that people want advice on something so important. After all, people get advice and help on buying homes and cars, and even on their wardrobe or hair color; so why not seek advice from someone who can explain your financial options and help you create a workable, understandable savings plan? And if you choose to seek out a professional advisor, please perform careful due diligence before making your selection.

Amidst all of this, it is important to note that there is some positive news, and not everyone is ignoring his or her retirement. In the Gallup survey, 30% said they have a plan. People were more likely to have a plan if they had a college degree (38%) or if they made more than $75,000 a year (43%).[200]

---

[200] DeGroot, Michael. (3 June 2013). *New Gallup poll shows two-thirds of Americans do not budget*. Deseret News. Retrieved from http://www.deseretnews.com/article/865581100/New-Gallup-poll-shows-two-thirds-of-Americans-do-not-budget.html?pg=all

Painless Savings

Saving money doesn't have to be painful. I urge you to sit down and write an honest list of all your spending: restaurants, clothes, salons, tuition, medical care, supermarkets, prescriptions, Uber, vacations, personal trainers, cell phones, cable TV, entertainment, and so on. For just one month, spend as you normally do and make a note of each expense, put each receipt into an envelope or review your credit card statement. "Tally up" at the end of the month. This will help you remember where the money went. I'm not asking you to deny yourself what you want, but I do want you to know where your money is going so that you can see where you might be able to save more.

Make it a game. How much can you save in three months? Six months? A year? How much more can you save if you give up drinking soda, smoking cigarettes, or that Starbucks morning latte? Get creative. It can be fun to find more cost-effective alternatives to the things you thought you couldn't do without. You may find new interests along the way.

Millennials, if they start to save early, have the advantage of benefitting from more years of compounding growth. For instance, if you decide to eat pizza once a week instead of dining at pricey sit-down restaurants, you may potentially save around $50 per week. If you automatically invest this $50, and if it earns an 8% rate compounded weekly for 37 years, your weekly savings could grow to roughly $593,000![201] This demonstrates the benefit of compounding and, particularly, how Millennials have time on their side. Little

---

[201] *Examples provided herein are for informational purposes only and do not reflect actual results and are not guarantees of future results. Actual results will vary and fluctuate with market conditions. All investments involve risk. Fluctuations in the financial markets and other factors may cause declines in the value of your account.

things can add up. So find some painless savings, and invest them wisely; it might make a huge difference 30 or 40 years down the line.

Regardless of your age, you may have some kind of "leak" in your savings plan that you can plug effectively once you locate it. This is what Charles and Leslie Dougherty discovered when they looked at their cash flow. Initially, they hadn't planned to dine out a lot when they started living aboard their sailboat. It wasn't until they realized they'd spent $2,000 in one month on expensive restaurants that they stepped back and reevaluated their priorities. They simply began cooking more and dining out less. Even in retirement, the concept of painless savings can be helpful.

Whether it is the daily latte, visits to a local bar, or going out to dinner several nights a week, look at one expense that isn't essential, and commit to automatically shifting that to your monthly savings. Over time, that can make a real difference.

Understand How Money Can Work For or Against You: The Impact of Compound Interest

We can see that compound *growth* on our investments can be beneficial, but we also need to understand that compound *interest* can work against us when we are borrowing money. This is why it is important to avoid the spending traps that I explained in chapter 5. To be clear, if you are carrying consumer debt, you might be setting back your financial plans. Let's look at the cost of debt.

Interest

Interest is the money a person or company pays regularly at a particular rate for the use of money lent to them or for delaying the repayment of a debt. More simply put, interest is the cost of using other people's money. If you don't have money, you can borrow it, but you'll pay for the privilege. That $60,000 BMW or SUV you want will cost you $60,000 if you pay cash; however, if you borrow the money, you'll need to pay interest, and depending on your credit scores and other factors, your rate will vary. Keep in mind, consumer debt is not tax deductible.

Basically, the two major criteria to setting interest rates are the riskiness of the investment and the lender's cost of money. The part of this equation that you can control is your credit rating. People with a good credit rating tend to be considered lower risk and therefore receive a more favorable interest rate when borrowing money, relative to someone who has a lower credit rating. This is another reason why good habits when you are young will benefit you later!

How Compound Interest Works

Compound interest is like "interest on your interest." Compound interest can work for you, as we saw above, when you're earning interest on your savings. But compound interest works *against* you if you're accruing interest on debt. Take for instance credit card debt. A credit card balance of $20,000 carried at an interest rate of 20% (compounded monthly) would result in a total compound interest of $4,388 over one year or about $365 per month. If you have several credit cards with similar balances, you can see how quickly you can get into serious financial difficulties by not paying off the cards every month.

The formula for calculating compound interest is:

> Compound Interest = Total amount of Principal and Interest in Future (or Future Value) *less* Principal amount at present (or Present Value).

$$= [P(1+i)^n] - P$$
$$= P[(1+i)^n - 1]$$

(Where P = Principal, i = nominal annual interest rate in percentage terms, and n = number of compounding periods.)

If the number of compounding periods is more than once per year, "i" and "n" must be adjusted accordingly. The "i" must be divided by the number of compounding periods per year, and "n" is the number of compounding periods per year × the loan or investments maturity period in years.[202]

For example:

- The compound interest on $10,000 compounded annually at 10% (i = 10%) for 10 years (n = 10) = $25,937.42 - $10,000 = $15,937.42.

- The amount of compound interest on $10,000 compounded monthly at 10% (i = 0.833%) for 10 years (n = 120) = $27,070.41 - $10,000 = $17,070.41.

As you can see, the interest debt that is compounded monthly is more costly than the debt that is compounded annually, in this case. This is a good reminder that it is important to understand the true cost of your liabilities. "Prudence" is the watchword when using credit cards and taking on consumer debt.

---

[202] *Compound Interest* (n.d.). Investopedia. Retrieved from http://www.investopedia.com/terms/c/compoundinterest.asp (accessed 29 June 2016).

The Results of Not Funding Your Retirement

What you want to avoid is working hard your entire life and, because of not saving adequately, finding yourself unable to enjoy life on your own terms. When you are retirement age, you will appreciate being able to work only if you want to, not because you need to.

However, many people are facing an underfunded retirement due to inadequate savings. This creates declines in standard of living among seniors and will also have a societal impact.

Take, for example, seniors who decide to live together as they grow older. Women, with their longer life expectancies than men, are the gender that we more often see cohabitating in their senior years to offset costs like transportation, rent, and home maintenance. They gather together in apartments or houses called "Golden Girl Homes." This term was a result of the 1990s television show called "The Golden Girls." This very popular sitcom addressed more than just social issues. It highlighted the financial struggles of four, single, comfortably middle-class women over the age of 50. The women were either divorced or widowed and lived together in a home in Miami in order to share the high costs of city living. While the differences in their personalities and events in their lives made for an entertaining sitcom, the show was based on a very real premise: older, single—and, yes, middle-class—women often can have a hard time making it on their own financially. Here we had an early version of the "sharing economy," which often involves the *sharing* of larger assets such as cars (think Uber) and houses (think Airbnb).

The Golden Girls theme has actually become a real-life solution for many seniors trying to manage on a middle-class, fixed income. This is a reality for many people, as evidenced by the record 57 million Americans (18.1% of the population of the United States) who were living in multigenerational family households in 2012. That's double the number who lived in such households in 1980.[203]

If the idea of sharing your home doesn't appeal to you, that's all the more motivation to start early by creating a strong written financial plan and being persistent in implementing it. Then, as a result of automatically saving a set monthly amount, combined with the benefit of compounding interest, you will have a good start toward achieving your personal financial goals while still enjoying life!

A Call to Action

I have described the daunting challenges facing the middle class. In the face of flat to declining real wages, an increasing tax burden, and higher health-care costs, it is becoming more difficult to find extra income at the end of the month to save. But what steps can be taken to turn around the decrease in financial wellness? As a nation, we need income to grow so that our workers earn sufficient wages. At a minimum, wages need to track or outpace inflation and hopefully rise with productivity gains. But how to do this as a nation is an enormous macroeconomic challenge. If we think this will come about through one perfectly written piece of legislation, we might be disappointed.

This is a complex problem. Our country needs a *combination of things* that will alert individuals to the financial reality they are facing. Individuals need to understand that they each are responsible for their own financial freedom and how challenging that is to attain. We also need early financial education in the home, mainstream financial literacy programs starting at a young age, and government funding

---

[203] Fry Richard & Jeffrey S. Passel. (17 July 2014). *Social & Demographic Trends.* Pew Research Center. http://www.pewsocialtrends.org/2014/07/17/in-post-recession-era-young-adults-drive-continuing-rise-in-multi-generational-living/

for a public awareness campaign much like those on public health and safety issues. Furthermore, our economy is likely to benefit when an entrepreneurial spirit is allowed to flourish in a smart, growth-promoting regulatory environment. People should not look to the government for middle-class financial freedom. The government should and will help the neediest and least fortunate among us, of course; that is any wealthy nation's minimum responsibility. But middle-class financial freedom falls on each individual to attain for him or herself.

Nations that have tried to create a workers' paradise have been some of the most dismal failures in world history. We have seen the pain and failure of communism, so the idea that a central government can build and deliver middle-class wealth is a fallacy. Governments can and should foster an economic environment that allows for a middle class to flourish in a thriving free market, while encouraging and educating individuals to be financially independent. Our strength as a nation depends on it. Without a strong middle class, we will have too wide of a gap between the lower and the upper classes, and none of us want that. Without a vibrant middle, those at the bottom rungs of the socioeconomic strata will have less of a vision to aim for, and therefore, a harder time transcending their economic class. Historically, each generation of Americans has worked for a chance to achieve a better lifestyle. We need this dream to be open to everyone, and we also need it for our nation to remain the world's premier economic engine.

Financial literacy needs to become something that permeates all communities, regardless of demographics or socioeconomic standing. Further, these concepts must speak to families, especially those with children, at the youngest ages possible. In other words, financial literacy should be commonplace, known to all, and incorporated into school curriculums, media campaigns, library shelves and, most importantly, ongoing parental discussions.

I hope that this book has provided you with the beginnings of a roadmap to financial freedom. The next step is for you to take action. It's about taking one small step today, another tomorrow, and then continuing each day. This is often the best way to move from just working each day with no plan to working purposefully and gaining your financial freedom.

My deepest hope is that you take control of your financial life. By doing so you will have more financial freedom and personal choice—two things that money *can* help buy and two things worth your effort. In the meantime, I wish you all the best on your journey!

Appendix A

Calculation to Determine
What is Your Unique Formula?

$$PRI = \left\{ CRS*(1+R)^N + MS\left[\frac{\left(1+\left(\frac{R}{12}\right)\right)^{N*12}-1}{\left(\frac{R}{12}\right)}\right] + EI*(1+R)^{N-n} \right\} * SWR + P + SSI$$

Key Variables:

　　PRI = Projected Retirement Income
　　EAR = Expected Assets at Retirement
　　SWR = Sustainable Withdrawal Rate
　　CRS = Current Retirement Savings
　　MS = Monthly Savings
　　EI = Expected Inheritance
　　P = Annual Pension Amount
　　SSI = Social Security Income
　　R = Growth Rate less Inflation Rate
　　N = Number of Years to Retirement
　　n = Number of Years until Receipt of Inheritance

5 Step Process for Determining What is Your Unique Formula?™

To determine your Projected Retirement Income (PRI) use this handy five-step process. (1) Find the FV of Current Retirement Savings (CRS), (2) find the FV of Monthly Savings (MS), (3) find the FV of Expected Inheritance (EI), (4) find your Expected Assets at Retirement (EAR), (5) calculate your Projected Retirement Income (PRI).

Below is a hypothetical example of how you calculate Projected Retirement Income.

SWR = 4%
CRS = $400,000
MS = $1,000
EI = $250,000
P = $0
SSI = $25,000
R = 5%
N = 20
n = 10

Step 1: Find the FV of Current Retirement Savings (CRS)

$FV\ CRS = CRS * (1 + R)^N$
$FV\ CRS = 400{,}000 * (1 + 0.05)^{20}$
$FV\ CRS = \$1{,}061{,}319.08$

Step 2: Find the FV of Monthly Savings (MS)

$$FV\ MS = MS\left[\frac{\left(1+\left(\frac{R}{12}\right)\right)^{N*12}-1}{\left(\frac{R}{12}\right)}\right]$$

$$FV\ MS = 1{,}000\left[\frac{\left(1+\left(\frac{0.05}{12}\right)\right)^{20*12}-1}{\left(\frac{0.05}{12}\right)}\right]$$

FV MS = $411,033.67

Step 3: Find the FV of Expected Inheritance (EI)

$FV\ EI = EI * (1 + R)^N$
$FV\ EI = 250{,}000 * (1 + 0.05)\ (20 - 10)$
$FV\ EI = \$407{,}223.66$

Step 4: Find the Expected Assets at Retirement (EAR) by adding the future values calculated in steps 1 through 3.

$EAR = FV\ CRS + FV\ MS + FV\ EI$
$EAR = 1{,}061{,}319.08 + 411{,}033.67 + 407{,}223.66$
$EAR = \$1{,}879{,}576.41$

Step 5: Find the Projected Retirement Income (PRI) by multiplying the Expected Assets at Retirement (EAR) by the Sustainable Withdrawal Rate (SWR), and then add any estimated annual Pension (P) and Social Security Income (SSI).

PRI = EAR * SWR + P + SSI
PRI = 1,879,576.41 * 0.04 + 0 + 25,000
PRI = $100,183.06

This is for informational and educational purposes only and is not intended to provide investment advice. This formula is used to provide a rough approximation and may not reflect your actual result. We cannot and do not guarantee its applicability or accuracy in regards to your individual circumstances. We are not responsible for the consequences of any decisions or actions taken in reliance upon or as a result of the information provided by this formula. We are not responsible for any human errors or omissions.

Appendix B

Sample Cash Flow Worksheet

	CURRENT	SEMI-RETIREMENT	RETIREMENT
Monthly Net Income After 401(k) Contributions	$	$	$
Monthly Income from Inheritance / Trust Funds / Pensions	$	$	$
Monthly Net Cash Flow from Investment	$	$	$
Real Estate (After All Expenses)			
Monthly Cash Flow From Other Sources	$	$	$
Alimony or Child Support RECEIVED	$	$	$
Total Monthly Income (excluding reinvested Dividends & Interest)	$	$	$
Mortgage Including PITI (Principal Interest Taxes Interest) or Rent on Primary Residence	$	$	$

	CURRENT	SEMI-RETIREMENT	RETIREMENT
Mortgage (PITI) or Renton Secondary Residence / Vacation Home	$	$	$
Mortgage (PITI) or Renton All Other Real Estate	$	$	$
Repairs, Cleaning, Landscaping, Condo Fees, etc. (Primary Residence)	$	$	$
Repairs, Cleaning, Landscaping, Condo Fees, etc. (Secondary Residence /Vacation Home)	$	$	$
Repairs, Cleaning, Landscaping, Condo Fees, etc. (All Other Real Estate)	$	$	$
Furniture / Remodeling (All Real Estate)	$	$	$
All Utility, Internet, Cable Payments	$	$	$
Phone / Cell Phones	$	$	$
Fitness Clubs / Country Club / Memberships	$	$	$
Day Care / Summer Camps	$	$	$
Private School / College (include current investments for future costs)	$	$	$
Auto Payment(s) - All Lease or Loan Payments	$	$	$
Gas, Maintenance and Repairs on Auto	$	$	$
Auto Insurance	$	$	$

	CURRENT	SEMI-RETIREMENT	RETIREMENT
Metro / Parking / Taxies / Limo / Uber	$	$	$
Health Insurance (only if paid w/ after-tax $'s)	$	$	$
Out of Pocket Health Care Costs	$	$	$
Support of Elderly Parents / Relatives	$	$	$
Life / Disability / Long Term Care Insurance	$	$	$
Financial / Legal / CPA / Professional Fees	$	$	$
Alimony Expense	$	$	$
Clothing Purchases	$	$	$
Dry Cleaning	$	$	$
Supermarket	$	$	$
Pharmacy / Personal Care	$	$	$
Salon / Cosmetic Services	$	$	$
Restaurants / Lunches	$	$	$
Entertainment	$	$	$
Vacations (include all related, e.g., Air, Hotel, Meals, etc.)	$	$	$
Gifts / Presents	$	$	$
Charity / Tithing	$	$	$
Miscellaneous / OTHER	$	$	$
(Less) Total Monthly Expenses	$	$	$
Surplus Available For Investing	$	$	$

CPSIA information can be obtained
at www.ICGtesting.com
Printed in the USA
FFHW021819031218
49748191-54195FF